THE USBORNE BOOK OF
BIG MACHINES

Harriet Castor, Clive Gifford
& Caroline Young

Designed by Will Dawes
Edited by Felicity Parker

Illustrated by
Andy Burton, Mark Franklin,
Teri Gower, Nick Hawker, Chris Lyon,
Dheeraj Verma & Sean Wilkinson

Digital imaging by Mike Olley

Consultants: James Allen, Jon Barrance, L. F. E. Coombs, Andrew Gaved, Gibb Grace,
George Hosford, Mick Roberts, Quentin Spurring, D. Wheeler & Steve Williams.

With special thanks to Renault UK Ltd.

THE USBORNE BOOK OF
BIG MACHINES

DiGGERS & CRANES

Bulldozers

Bulldozers clear the ground ready for building. They push earth, stones and tree stumps out of their way with a huge metal blade. This is called dozing.

This bulldozer has a powerful engine. It can push things much heavier than itself.

Crawler tracks

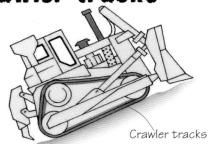

Crawler tracks

Crawler tracks help the heavy bulldozer climb up steep banks.

They can go over bumps more smoothly than wheels, too.

They also help stop the bulldozer from sinking into soft, muddy ground.

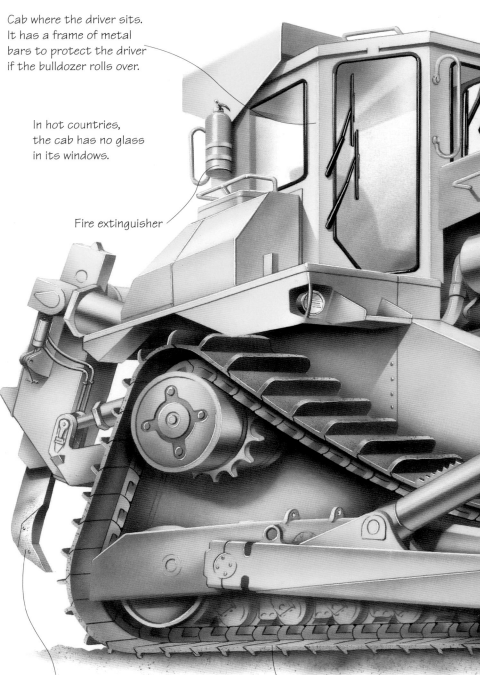

Cab where the driver sits. It has a frame of metal bars to protect the driver if the bulldozer rolls over.

In hot countries, the cab has no glass in its windows.

Fire extinguisher

This tool is called a ripper. It is dragged behind the bulldozer to break up hard, stony ground.

Metal crawler tracks cover the bulldozer's wheels.

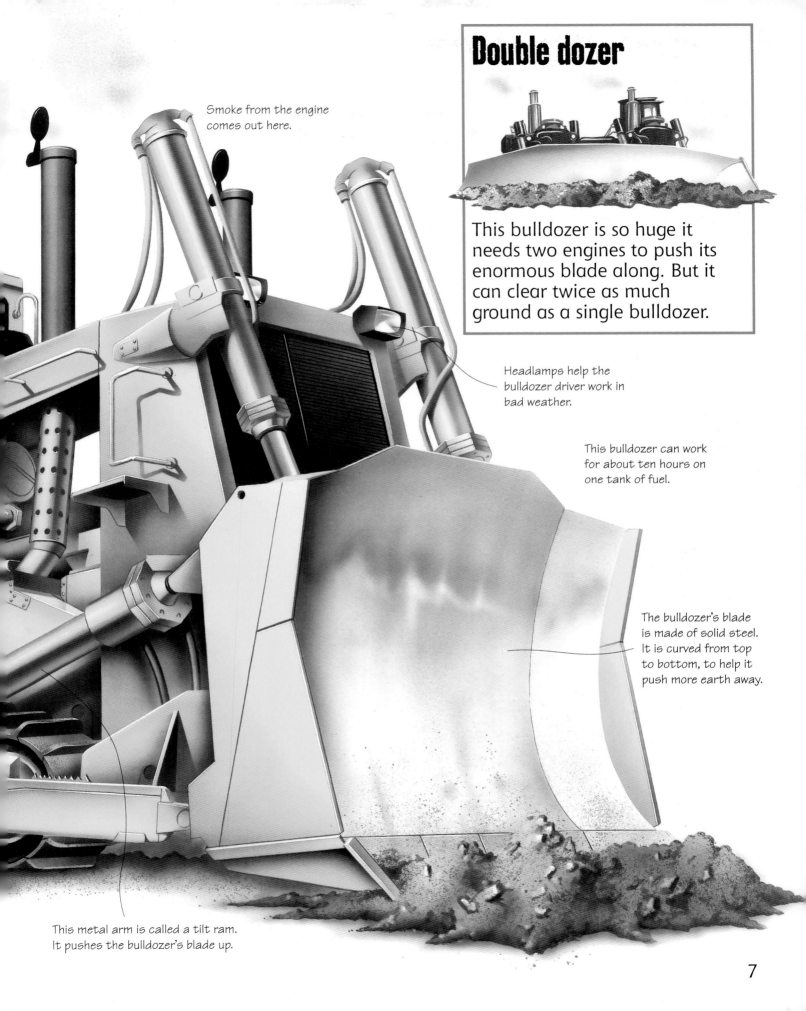

Smoke from the engine comes out here.

This bulldozer is so huge it needs two engines to push its enormous blade along. But it can clear twice as much ground as a single bulldozer.

Headlamps help the bulldozer driver work in bad weather.

This bulldozer can work for about ten hours on one tank of fuel.

The bulldozer's blade is made of solid steel. It is curved from top to bottom, to help it push more earth away.

This metal arm is called a tilt ram. It pushes the bulldozer's blade up.

7

# Excavators

Excavators are digging machines and there are lots of different sorts. This one is a backhoe excavator. It digs into the ground with a metal bucket called a backhoe.

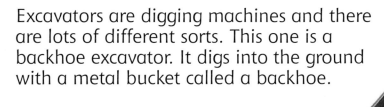

This is a ram. It slides in and out of its metal case and makes the excavator's arm move.

This backhoe can dig up more than 500 shovelfuls of earth at a time.

This long arm is known as the boom. The driver can make it shorter or longer for different digging jobs.

This is the dipper arm. It dips in and out of the ground as the excavator digs.

These metal teeth cut through the earth easily.

This mini-excavator is so small it could almost fit into the backhoe excavator's bucket. It does small digging jobs.

Other excavators

These excavators have tools that do many different jobs.

This excavator can carry earth in a loader bucket.

Claws help this excavator pick up pipes or logs.

This excavator has a metal grab which can pick things up easily.

Radio aerial

Control lever

Crawler tracks help
the excavator grip
wet, muddy ground.

Some excavators have
drills like this, called augers.

This excavator's split bucket can
bite chunks out of the earth.

Metal forks make a platform
to lift things up with.

9

Backhoe loader

This excavator can dig pits and trenches with a backhoe or scoop up and transport earth in a bucket called a loader.

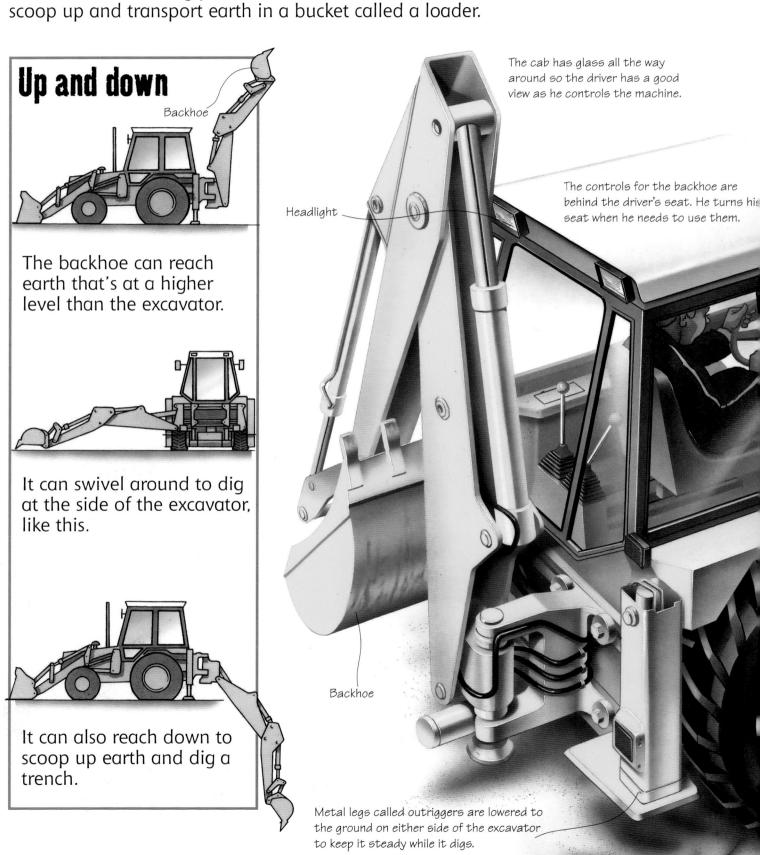

Up and down

Backhoe

The backhoe can reach earth that's at a higher level than the excavator.

It can swivel around to dig at the side of the excavator, like this.

It can also reach down to scoop up earth and dig a trench.

The cab has glass all the way around so the driver has a good view as he controls the machine.

The controls for the backhoe are behind the driver's seat. He turns his seat when he needs to use them.

Headlight

Backhoe

Metal legs called outriggers are lowered to the ground on either side of the excavator to keep it steady while it digs.

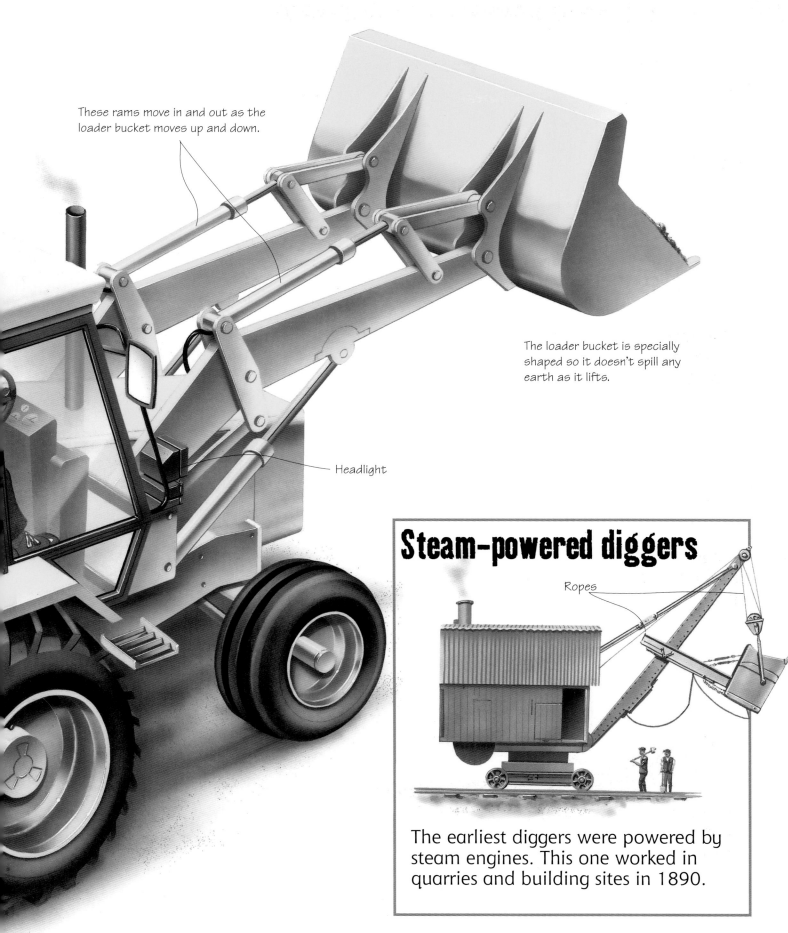

These rams move in and out as the loader bucket moves up and down.

The loader bucket is specially shaped so it doesn't spill any earth as it lifts.

Headlight

Steam-powered diggers

Ropes

The earliest diggers were powered by steam engines. This one worked in quarries and building sites in 1890.

Moving cranes

Truck cranes and crawler cranes move around on wheels or crawler tracks to travel quickly from job to job.

Ready to lift

Boom

The truck crane arrives at the building site with its boom folded up.

Outrigger

Metal legs called outriggers lift the crane off the ground.

The boom slowly lifts up and slides out ready to lift a load.

Truck crane

Truck cranes are built on the back of a truck. They have one cab for controlling the crane and one for driving the truck.

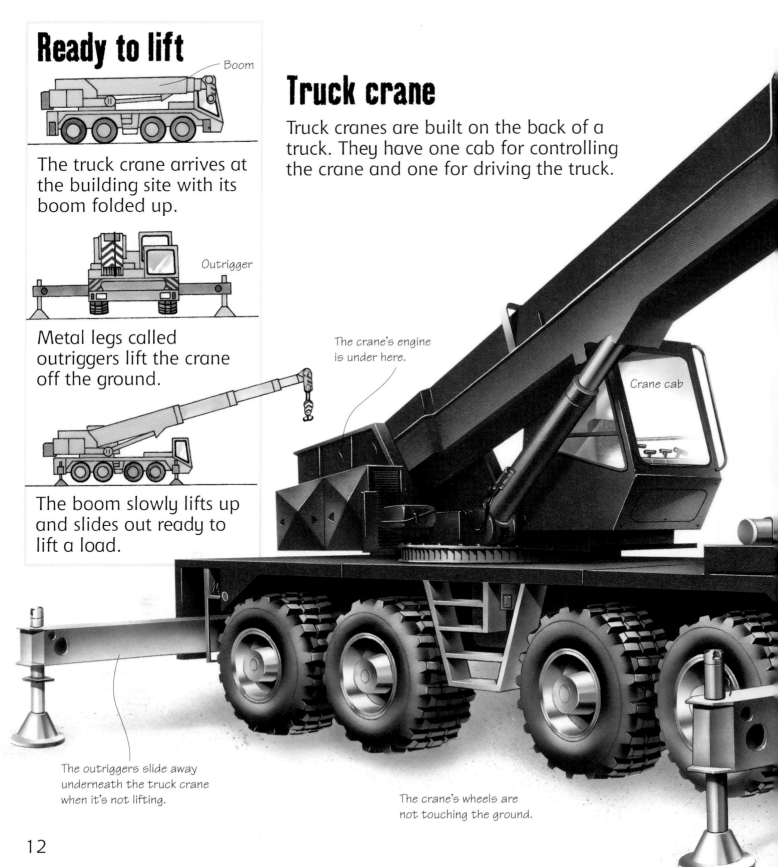

The crane's engine is under here.

Crane cab

The outriggers slide away underneath the truck crane when it's not lifting.

The crane's wheels are not touching the ground.

Inside a crane cab

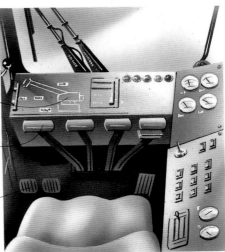

The dashboard shows the driver how much the load weighs.

Levers to control the crane

Pedals to raise and lower the boom

This boom is made of several parts that fit inside each other when the crane isn't lifting.

This boom can stretch up to the top of a six floor building.

The crane lifts loads with this steel hook.

Crawler crane

Crawler cranes have crawler tracks, like bulldozers. They can move while carrying heavy loads.

This boom can reach to the top of a 20 floor building.

Crawler cranes can only work on flat ground. If it's bumpy, they might topple over.

Truck cab

Crawler tracks

13

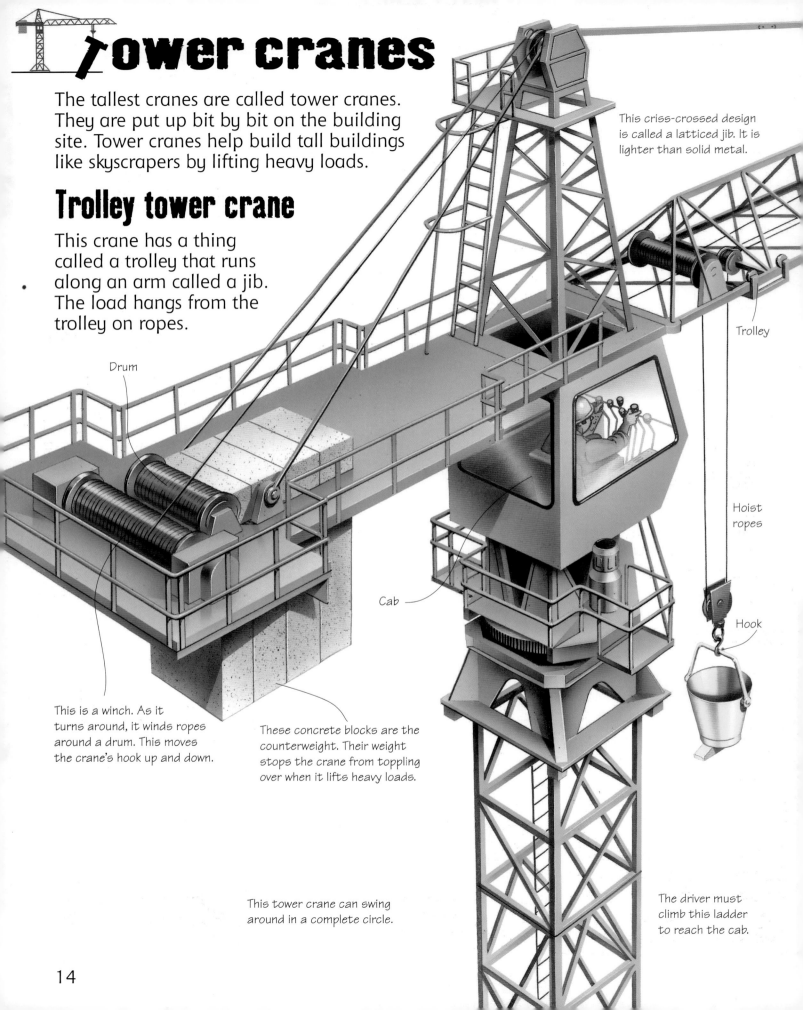

Tower cranes

The tallest cranes are called tower cranes. They are put up bit by bit on the building site. Tower cranes help build tall buildings like skyscrapers by lifting heavy loads.

Trolley tower crane

This crane has a thing called a trolley that runs along an arm called a jib. The load hangs from the trolley on ropes.

This criss-crossed design is called a latticed jib. It is lighter than solid metal.

Trolley

Drum

Hoist ropes

Cab

Hook

This is a winch. As it turns around, it winds ropes around a drum. This moves the crane's hook up and down.

These concrete blocks are the counterweight. Their weight stops the crane from toppling over when it lifts heavy loads.

This tower crane can swing around in a complete circle.

The driver must climb this ladder to reach the cab.

14

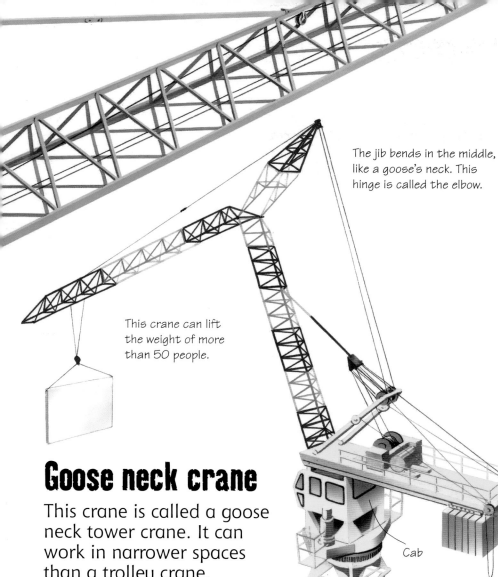

The jib bends in the middle, like a goose's neck. This hinge is called the elbow.

This crane can lift the weight of more than 50 people.

Goose neck crane

This crane is called a goose neck tower crane. It can work in narrower spaces than a trolley crane.

Cab

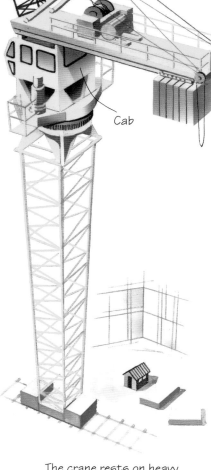

The crane rests on heavy metal rails. Concrete blocks hold it in place.

The first cranes

The first cranes were built by the Romans. Slaves ran around inside a wooden wheel with ropes tied to it. This lifted things up.

Bit by bit

Trucks bring the parts of the tower crane to the building site.

A truck crane lifts the pieces of the tower crane into place.

Builders bolt the bits of the crane's jib together on the ground.

Jib

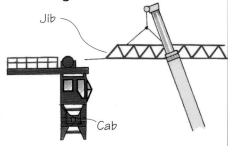

Cab

The cab and the jib are lifted into place by the truck crane.

Counterweight

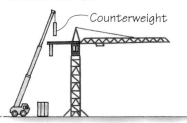

The truck crane lifts the counterweight. Now the crane is ready to work.

Building roads

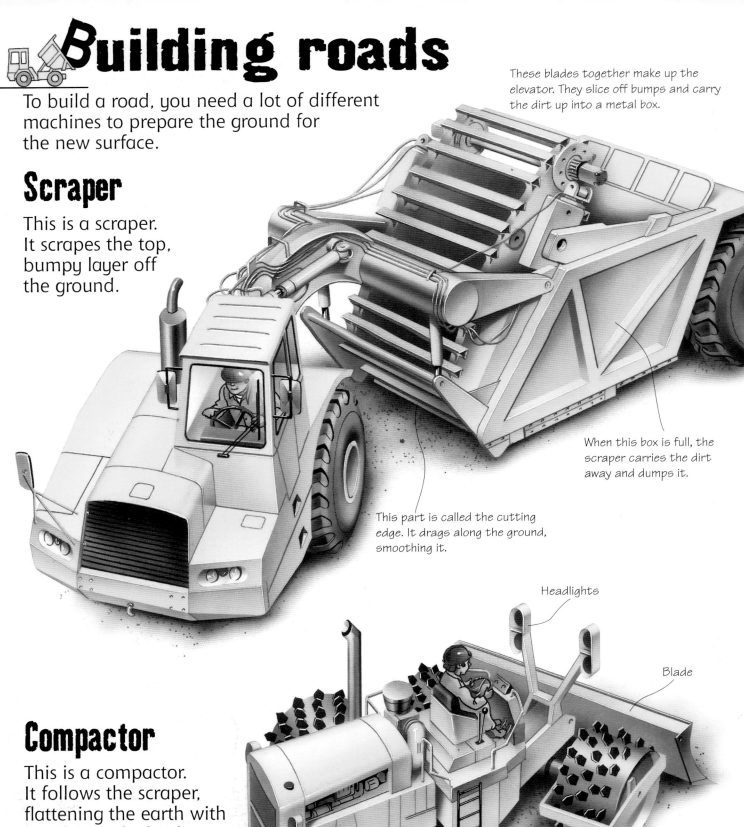

To build a road, you need a lot of different machines to prepare the ground for the new surface.

Scraper

This is a scraper. It scrapes the top, bumpy layer off the ground.

These blades together make up the elevator. They slice off bumps and carry the dirt up into a metal box.

When this box is full, the scraper carries the dirt away and dumps it.

This part is called the cutting edge. It drags along the ground, smoothing it.

Headlights

Blade

Compactor

This is a compactor. It follows the scraper, flattening the earth with heavy metal wheels.

The driver goes back and forth several times over the bumpy ground.

These wheels have little metal feet. They are sometimes called 'sheep's feet'.

When this dump truck is full, it weighs as much as five elephants.

Dump truck

This truck is called a dump truck. It's used for dumping small stones.

The stones will become the bottom layer of the new road.

This dump truck can dump its load of stones in 12 seconds.

This is an articulated dump truck. which means it can bend in the middle like this.

The back of the dump truck tips up to empty its load.

Grader

This is a grader. It smooths a flat layer of small stones over the ground, with its big metal blade.

This grader is about as long as a bus.

This blade is made of solid steel.

Surfacing roads

For surfacing roads, you need a paver and a roller. The paver lays a mixture of hot tar and small stones on the road. The roller makes sure the road is flat.

Roller

The roller drives slowly behind the paver, flattening the tar and stones with its heavy metal rollers.

It will go over the road several times to make it ready to drive on.

Steam rollers

The first rollers were called steam rollers. They had engines powered by steam and they were much slower. This one was built in about 1847.

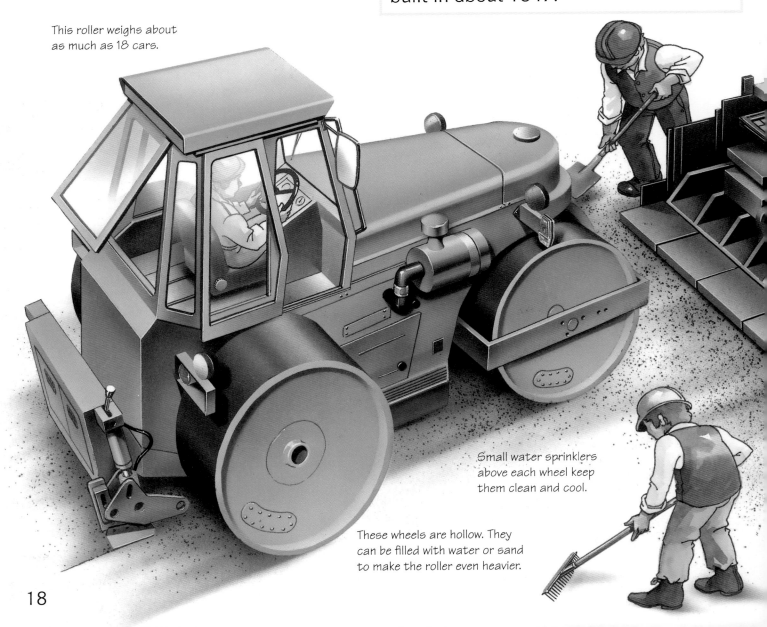

This roller weighs about as much as 18 cars.

Small water sprinklers above each wheel keep them clean and cool.

These wheels are hollow. They can be filled with water or sand to make the roller even heavier.

Paver

A paver spreads a layer of warm asphalt (a mixture of hot tar and small stones) over the road. It sets hard as it cools.

Filling up

A truck tips asphalt into a box called a hopper at the front of the paver.

As the paver drives along, the asphalt is fed through and comes out of the back.

The truck can fill the paver with asphalt while it works.

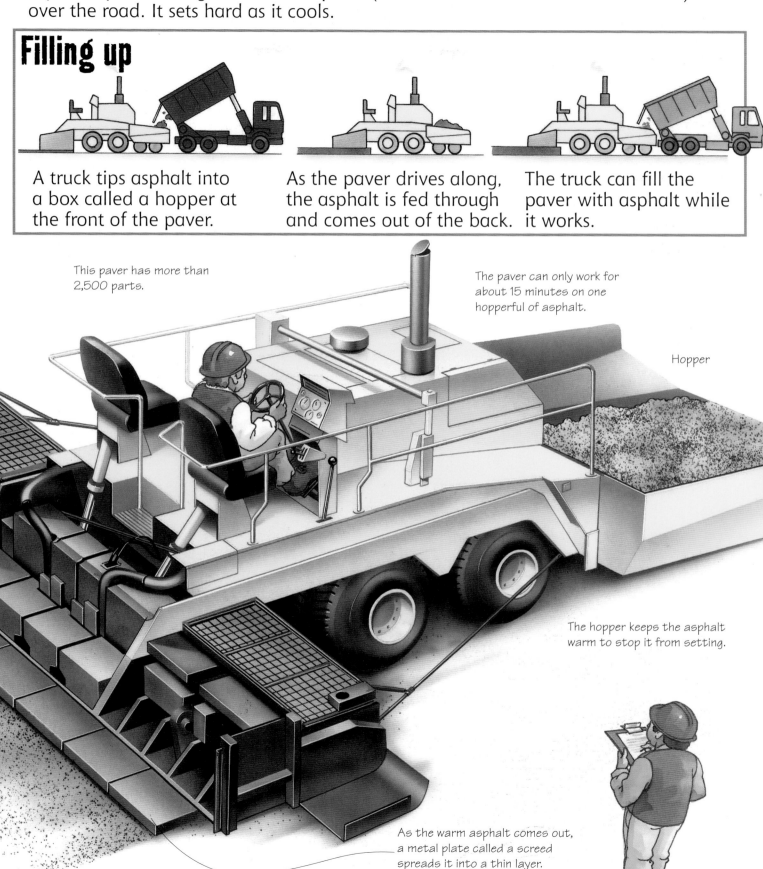

This paver has more than 2,500 parts.

The paver can only work for about 15 minutes on one hopperful of asphalt.

Hopper

The hopper keeps the asphalt warm to stop it from setting.

As the warm asphalt comes out, a metal plate called a screed spreads it into a thin layer.

19

Building machines

Tall buildings are very heavy so the ground beneath them has to be strong to hold them up. These building machines are used to drill holes and fill them with concrete and steel rods, to strengthen the ground.

Underground legs

First a crane drills a hole in the ground with a tool called an auger.

Then a truck crane lowers long steel rods down into each hole.

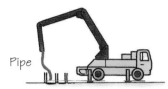

Finally, a concrete pump fills the holes with concrete.

Concrete mixer

Concrete is a mixture of chalk, stones, sand and water. They are mixed together in a big revolving drum inside a concrete mixer.

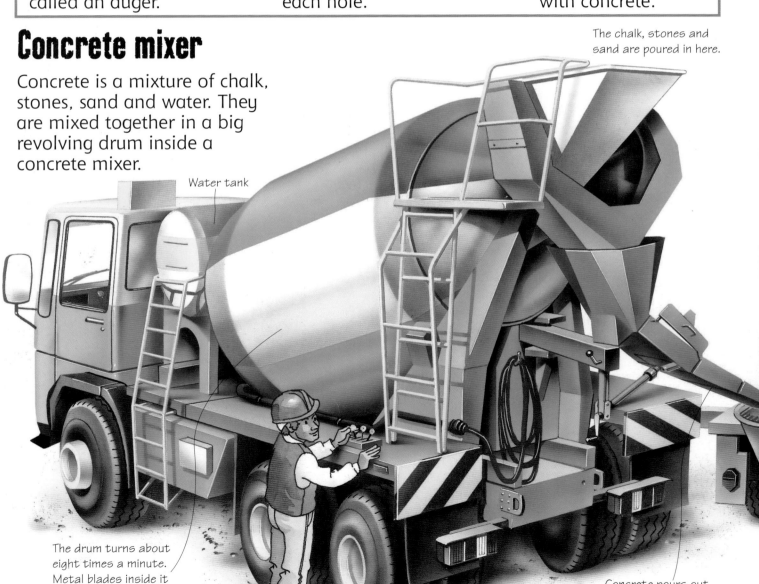

The chalk, stones and sand are poured in here.

Water tank

The drum turns about eight times a minute. Metal blades inside it mix the concrete.

Concrete pours out of this metal tube...

Mini-mixer

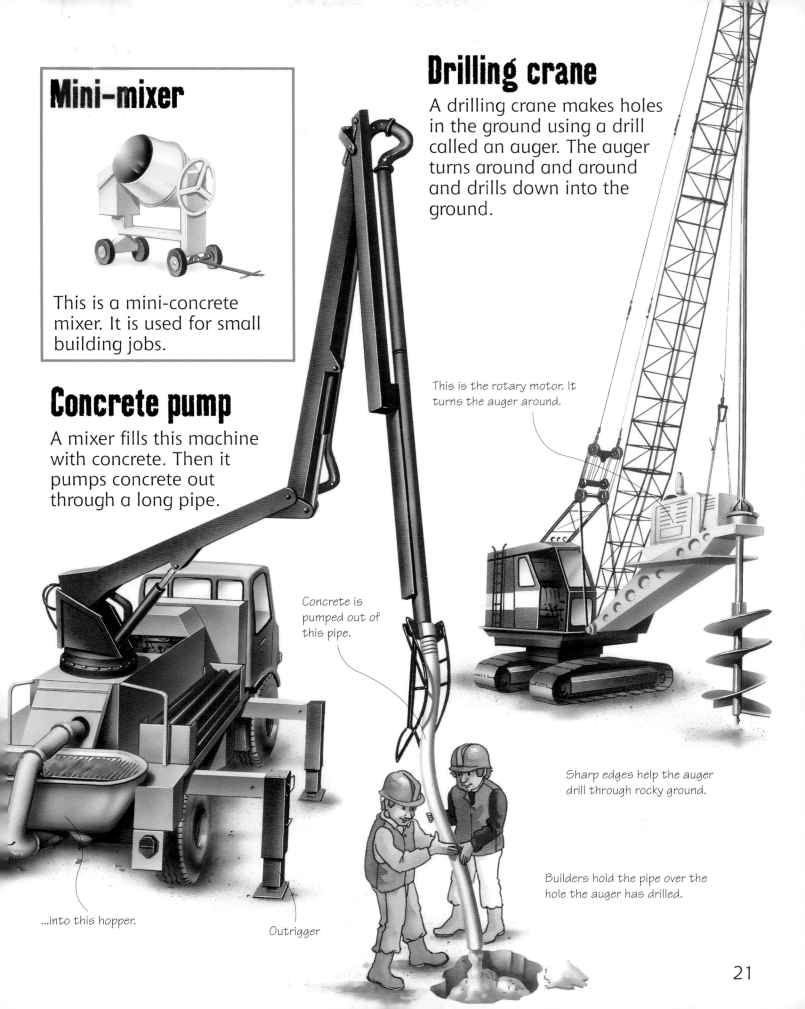

This is a mini-concrete mixer. It is used for small building jobs.

Concrete pump

A mixer fills this machine with concrete. Then it pumps concrete out through a long pipe.

...into this hopper.

Outrigger

Drilling crane

A drilling crane makes holes in the ground using a drill called an auger. The auger turns around and around and drills down into the ground.

This is the rotary motor. It turns the auger around.

Concrete is pumped out of this pipe.

Sharp edges help the auger drill through rocky ground.

Builders hold the pipe over the hole the auger has drilled.

21

Mining machines

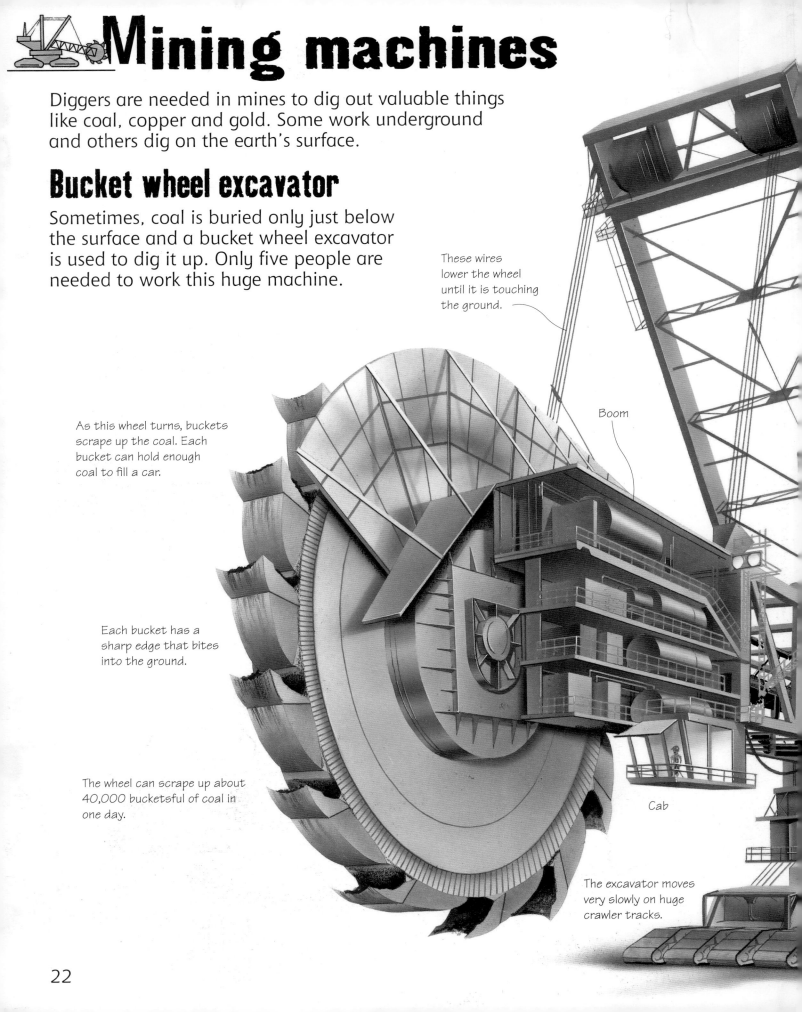

Diggers are needed in mines to dig out valuable things like coal, copper and gold. Some work underground and others dig on the earth's surface.

Bucket wheel excavator

Sometimes, coal is buried only just below the surface and a bucket wheel excavator is used to dig it up. Only five people are needed to work this huge machine.

These wires lower the wheel until it is touching the ground.

Boom

As this wheel turns, buckets scrape up the coal. Each bucket can hold enough coal to fill a car.

Each bucket has a sharp edge that bites into the ground.

The wheel can scrape up about 40,000 bucketsful of coal in one day.

Cab

The excavator moves very slowly on huge crawler tracks.

When they reach the top of the wheel, the buckets tip out their load. It falls onto a moving track inside the machine.

Underground mining

Coal and gold can also be found deep under the ground. Machines like these are used to dig them up.

Pick

This machine is called a continuous miner. It cuts coal off the wall of the mine with blades called picks.

This is a coal face cutter. It has sharp blades that slice coal off the walls of the tunnels inside mines.

The coal is carried along this moving track.

Coal falls off the end of the track onto these waiting railway trucks.

Floating diggers and cranes

Some diggers and cranes are built on top of boats so they can be used at sea, or on rivers.

Giant crane

This giant floating crane works at sea, sailing from job to job. About 350 men live and work on it.

These booms are so strong, they can lift whole ships.

There is a restaurant, hospital and entertainments on board.

The deck of this crane is as long as three swimming pools put end to end.

Helicopters land here, on the helipad, bringing people and equipment to the crane.

This hook is about twice as tall as a person.

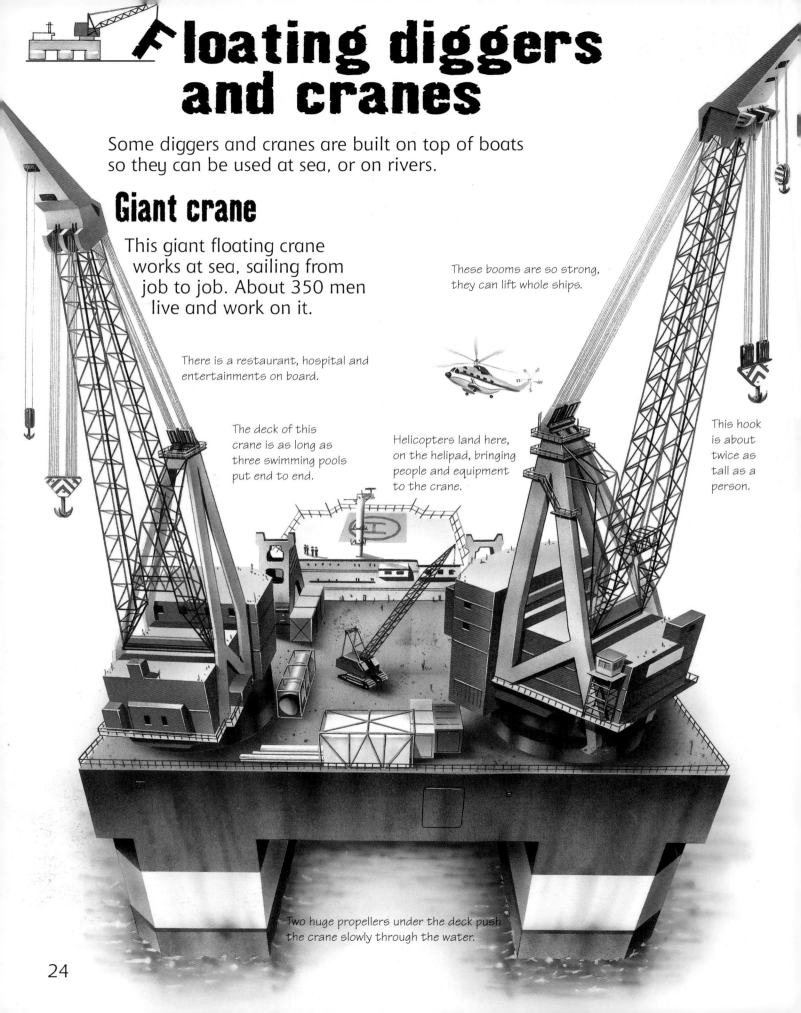

Two huge propellers under the deck push the crane slowly through the water.

Dredgers

Dredgers dig up mud and sand from the bottom of seas and rivers. This one is called a bucket dredger. It digs up mud using a chain of buckets called a ladder. They go around and around like a moving staircase.

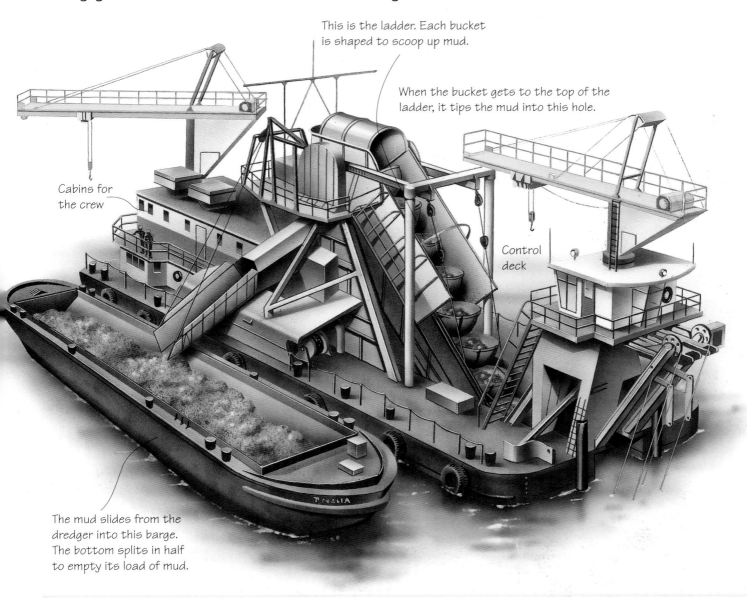

This is the ladder. Each bucket is shaped to scoop up mud.

When the bucket gets to the top of the ladder, it tips the mud into this hole.

Cabins for the crew

Control deck

The mud slides from the dredger into this barge. The bottom splits in half to empty its load of mud.

How a dredger works

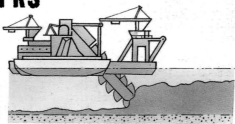

If mud builds up at the bottom of seas or rivers, ships can get stuck on it.

The dredger scoops up the mud and dumps it on a barge.

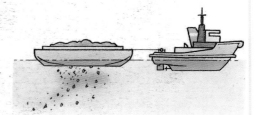

The barge carries it out to sea, and dumps it where the water is deep.

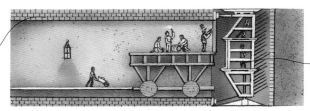

Tunnel diggers

Tunnelling machines have to be able to dig through earth, mud and even solid rock. The biggest ones are called Tunnel Boring Machines, or TBMs.

Early tunnels

Builders covered the inside of the tunnel with bricks.

This metal cage protected the men from falling earth.

This is one of the first tunnelling machines. It dug tunnels for underground trains in London nearly 200 years ago. As the machine moved forward, builders dug through earth with shovels at the front.

TBM

A TBM like this dug the Channel Tunnel under the sea between England and France.

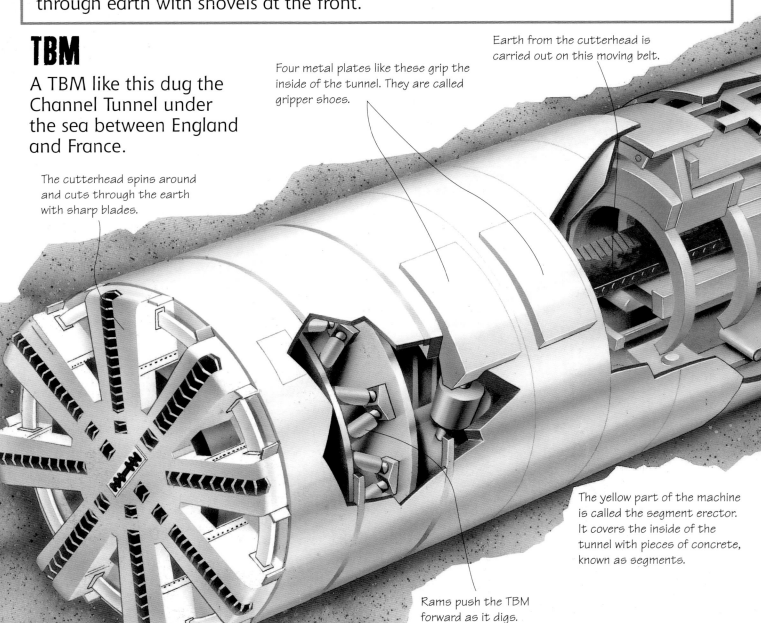

Four metal plates like these grip the inside of the tunnel. They are called gripper shoes.

Earth from the cutterhead is carried out on this moving belt.

The cutterhead spins around and cuts through the earth with sharp blades.

The yellow part of the machine is called the segment erector. It covers the inside of the tunnel with pieces of concrete, known as segments.

Rams push the TBM forward as it digs.

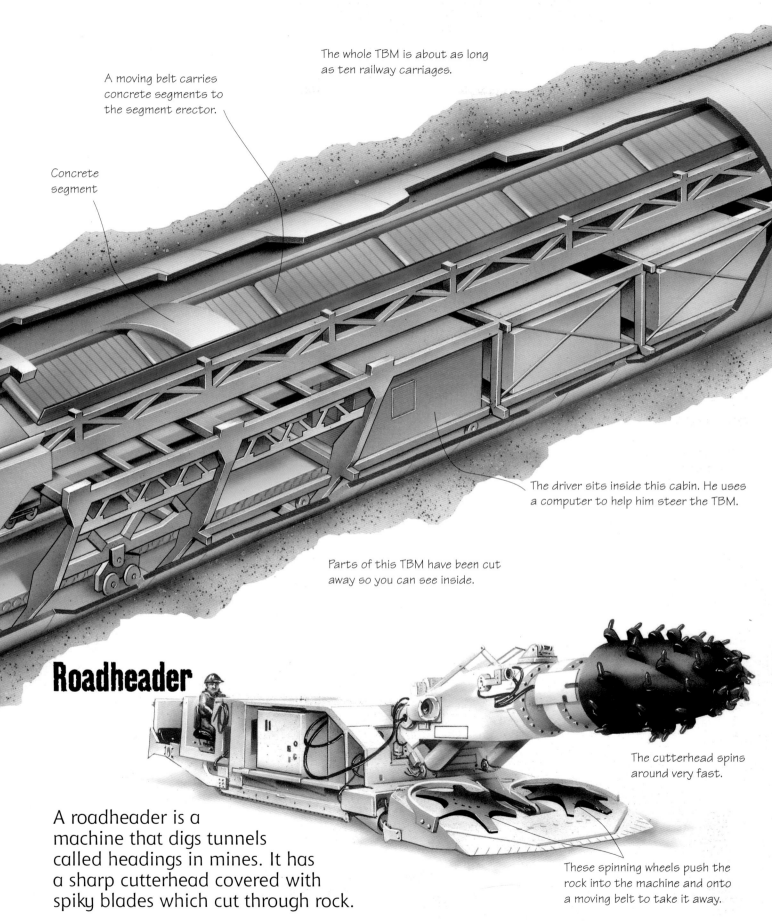

A moving belt carries concrete segments to the segment erector.

Concrete segment

The whole TBM is about as long as ten railway carriages.

The driver sits inside this cabin. He uses a computer to help him steer the TBM.

Parts of this TBM have been cut away so you can see inside.

Roadheader

A roadheader is a machine that digs tunnels called headings in mines. It has a sharp cutterhead covered with spiky blades which cut through rock.

The cutterhead spins around very fast.

These spinning wheels push the rock into the machine and onto a moving belt to take it away.

PLANES & HELICOPTERS

Planes in flight

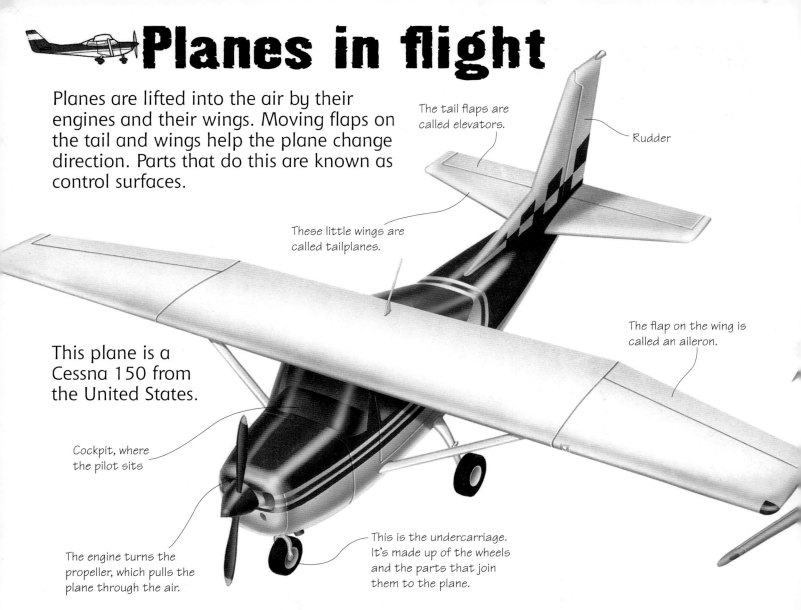

Planes are lifted into the air by their engines and their wings. Moving flaps on the tail and wings help the plane change direction. Parts that do this are known as control surfaces.

The tail flaps are called elevators.

Rudder

These little wings are called tailplanes.

The flap on the wing is called an aileron.

This plane is a Cessna 150 from the United States.

Cockpit, where the pilot sits

The engine turns the propeller, which pulls the plane through the air.

This is the undercarriage. It's made up of the wheels and the parts that join them to the plane.

What the control surfaces do

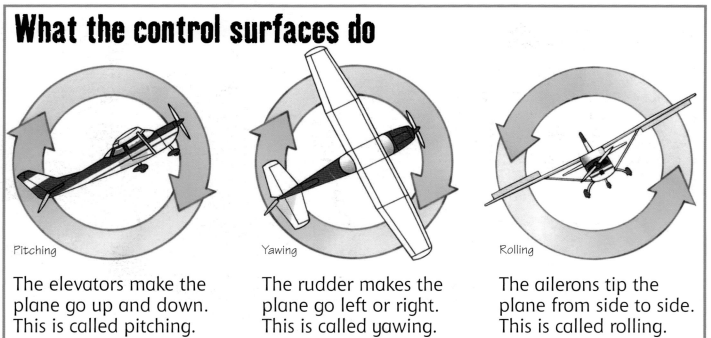

Pitching

Yawing

Rolling

The elevators make the plane go up and down. This is called pitching.

The rudder makes the plane go left or right. This is called yawing.

The ailerons tip the plane from side to side. This is called rolling.

Carrying passengers

Planes transport people all over the world. This plane, a BAe 146, can carry up to 110 passengers and their bags.

The body of a plane is called the fuselage.

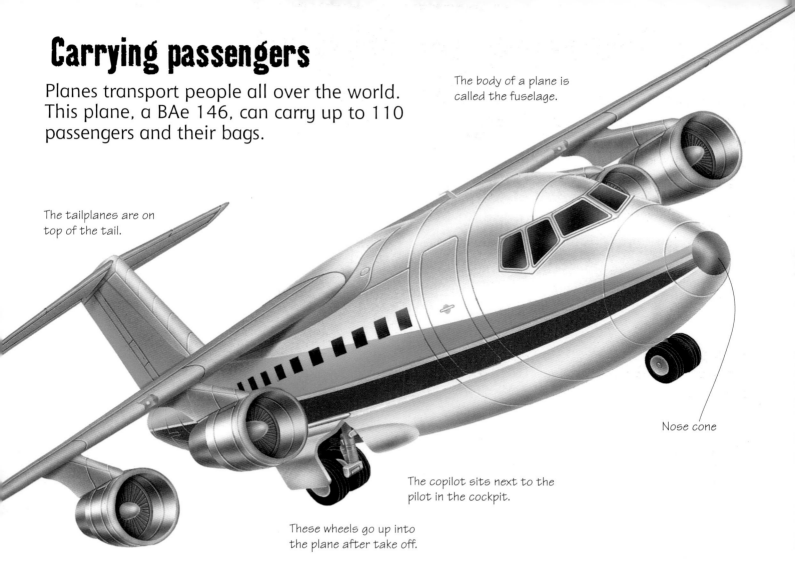

The tailplanes are on top of the tail.

Nose cone

The copilot sits next to the pilot in the cockpit.

These wheels go up into the plane after take off.

This plane has four jet engines. They push the plane forward.

Inside the cockpit

The cockpit contains all the controls the pilot needs to fly the plane. There are many dials and screens telling the pilot and copilot how the plane is doing.

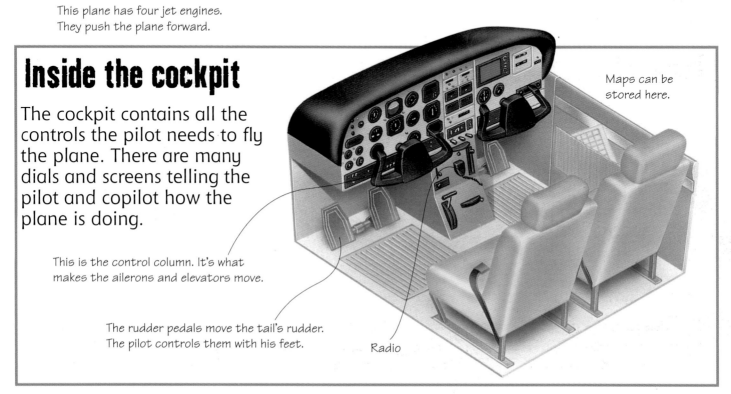

Maps can be stored here.

This is the control column. It's what makes the ailerons and elevators move.

The rudder pedals move the tail's rudder. The pilot controls them with his feet.

Radio

Helicopters

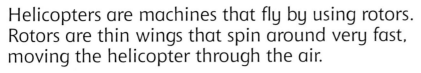

Helicopters are machines that fly by using rotors. Rotors are thin wings that spin around very fast, moving the helicopter through the air.

This is a German helicopter called an MBB-105.

There are seats inside for three passengers.

Dials and screens on the instrument panel inside the cockpit help the pilot fly the helicopter.

The rudder pedals control the tail rotor.

Many helicopters don't have wheels. These long, flat blades are called skids.

This lever is called the collective pitch control. It controls how high the helicopter flies.

The cabin door slides back.

What the main rotors do

Main rotors

The main rotors move a helicopter up, down, forward and back. A helicopter can fly straight up into the air. It only needs a small space to take off from.

Rotors tilted forward.

Helicopter flies forward.

A helicopter moves forward and back by tilting its main rotors. Helicopters can even stay still in the air. This is called hovering.

Rotor blades

The tail rotor helps the helicopter change direction.

This metal rod drives the tail rotor around. It is powered by the helicopter's engines.

The tailskid protects the tail if the helicopter leans back on the ground.

Left or right

The tail rotor steers the helicopter left or right.

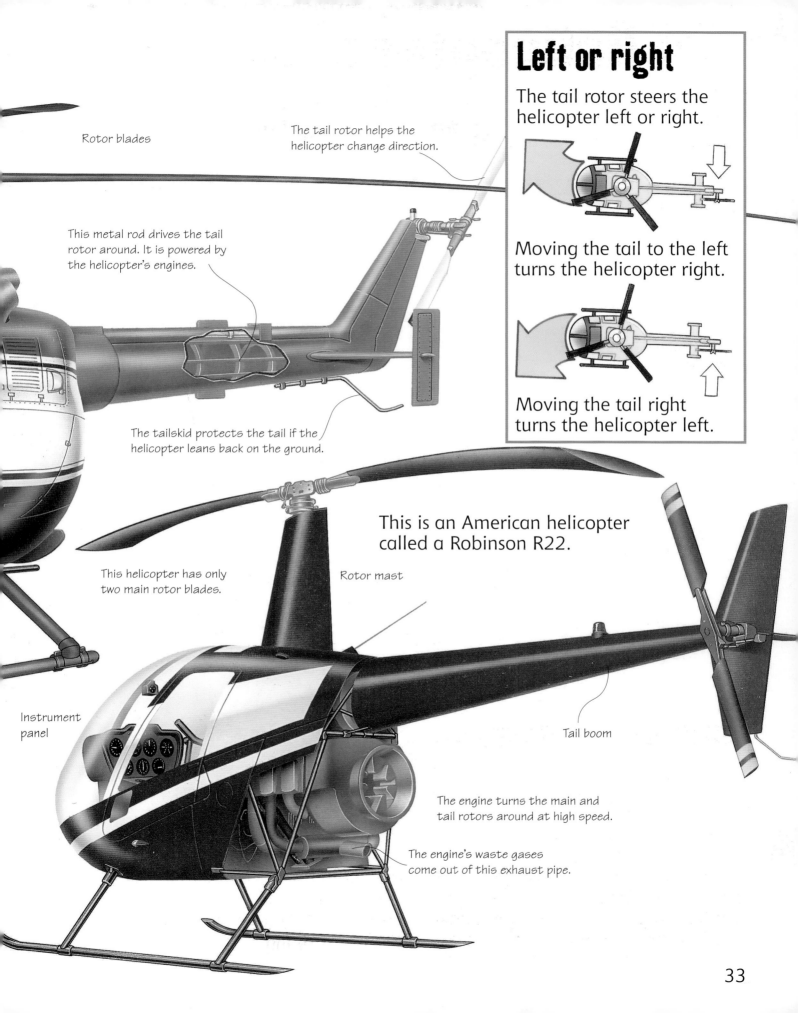

Moving the tail to the left turns the helicopter right.

Moving the tail right turns the helicopter left.

This is an American helicopter called a Robinson R22.

This helicopter has only two main rotor blades.

Rotor mast

Instrument panel

Tail boom

The engine turns the main and tail rotors around at high speed.

The engine's waste gases come out of this exhaust pipe.

33

Historic planes

The first plane flew in 1903. Since then, hundreds of different planes have been built. Here are four famous old planes.

The Blériot XI had a top speed of 75km/h (47mph). The engine in a modern family car is four times more powerful.

This plane was made of wood covered with light cloth.

A plane with only one set of wings is called a monoplane.

The Blériot XI

This plane was the first to cross the Channel between Britain and France. It was flown by Louis Blériot in 1909.

The engine came from an early motorcycle.

Fokker Dr.I triplane

This triplane is a famous plane from the First World War. Planes were first used to spot enemy troops, then they started to carry bombs and guns too.

A plane with three sets of wings is called a triplane.

Machine guns

This is the plane of a German fighter pilot called Baron von Richthofen. He was known as the Red Baron and was the most successful fighter pilot of the First World War.

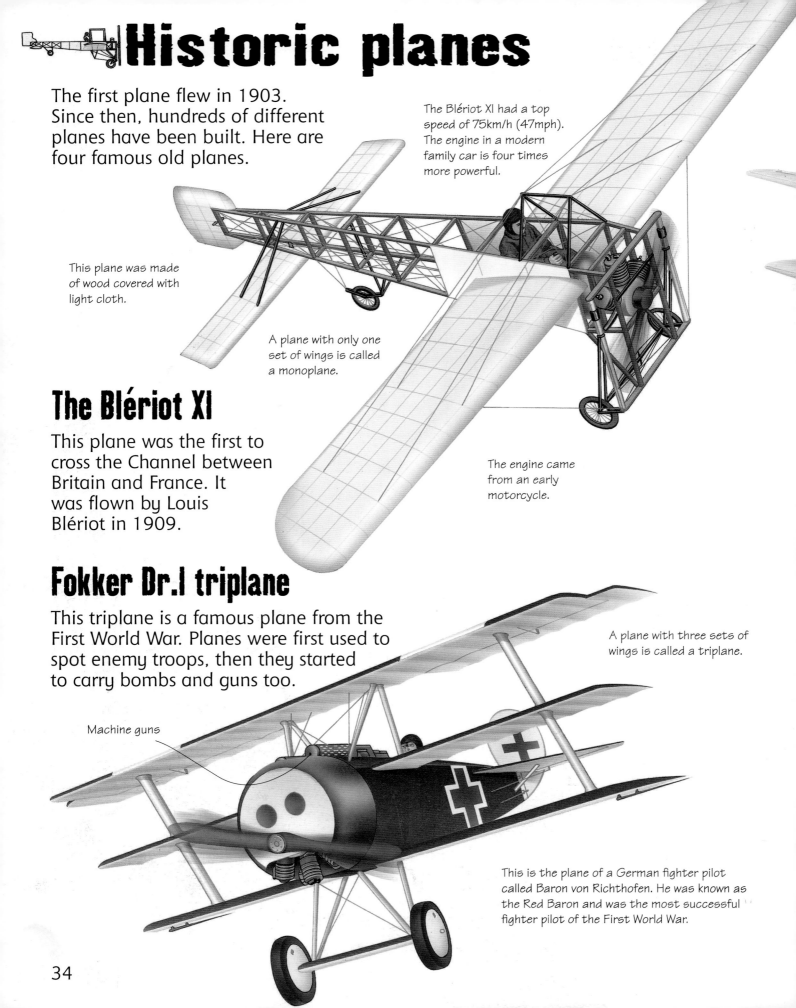

Dragon Rapide

This plane first flew in 1934. It helped to make flying more popular and was used by many different airlines. Inside there were seats for up to 16 people.

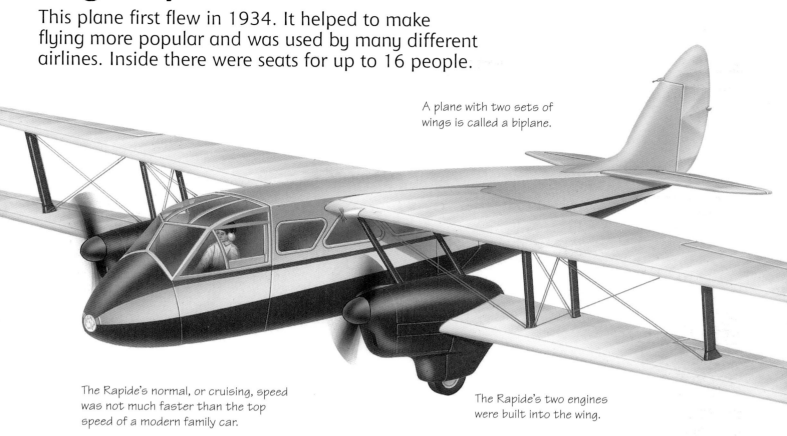

A plane with two sets of wings is called a biplane.

The Rapide's normal, or cruising, speed was not much faster than the top speed of a modern family car.

The Rapide's two engines were built into the wing.

Gloster Meteor

The Gloster Meteor was one of the earliest warplanes to be powered by a jet engine. It was built in Britain and first flew near the end of the Second World War.

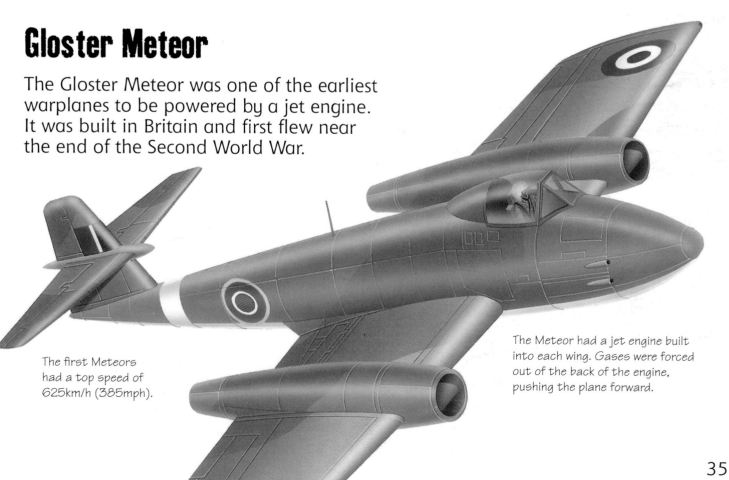

The first Meteors had a top speed of 625km/h (385mph).

The Meteor had a jet engine built into each wing. Gases were forced out of the back of the engine, pushing the plane forward.

Airliners

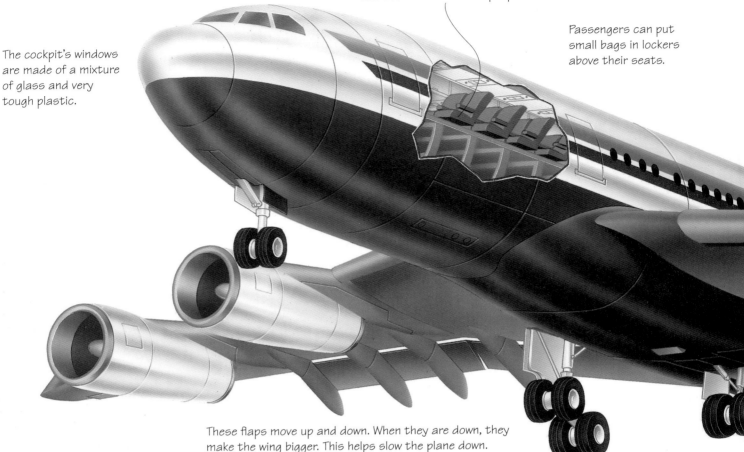

Planes that carry a lot of passengers are called airliners.

This airliner has been cut away so you can see inside. This is the passenger deck. It has seats for over 370 people.

Passengers can put small bags in lockers above their seats.

The cockpit's windows are made of a mixture of glass and very tough plastic.

These flaps move up and down. When they are down, they make the wing bigger. This helps slow the plane down.

Computers in the cockpit

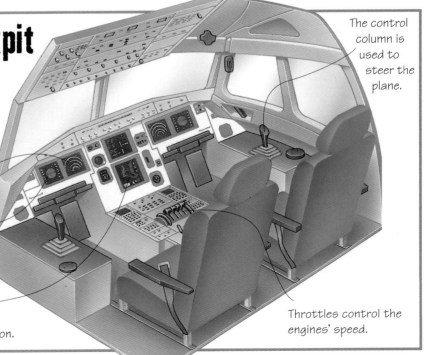

The A340's cockpit is full of screens and dials that tell the pilot about the plane's height and speed.

This screen shows if the plane is going up, down, left or right.

This screen shows a line called the artificial horizon. It tells the pilot if the plane is flying level.

A map is shown on this screen. This helps the pilot fly the plane in the right direction.

The control column is used to steer the plane.

Throttles control the engines' speed.

Airbus A340

The Airbus A340 is an airliner used by companies all over the world. It first flew in 1991 and over 300 have been built. It is full of high-tech equipment and has a cruising speed of over 900km/h (560mph).

Today, the fastest passenger airliner is the Boeing 747, which can travel at speeds of up to 974km/h (605mph).

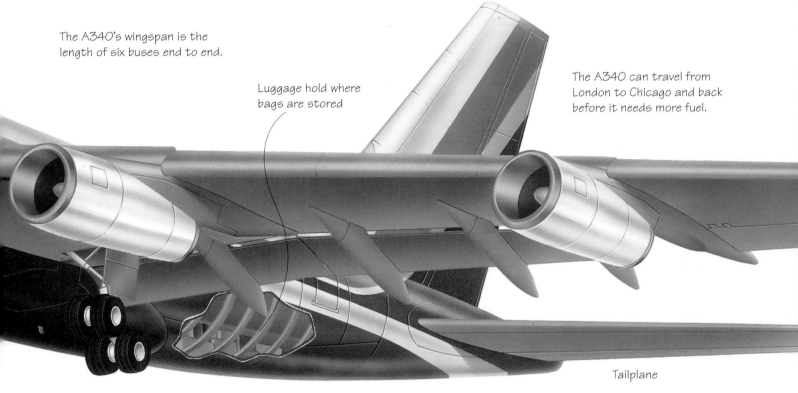

The A340's wingspan is the length of six buses end to end.

Luggage hold where bags are stored

The A340 can travel from London to Chicago and back before it needs more fuel.

Tailplane

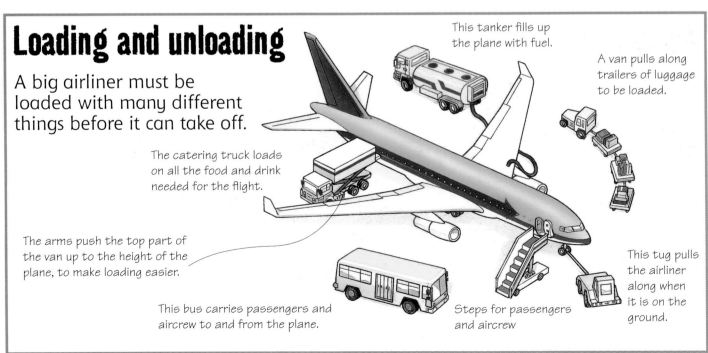

Loading and unloading

A big airliner must be loaded with many different things before it can take off.

This tanker fills up the plane with fuel.

A van pulls along trailers of luggage to be loaded.

The catering truck loads on all the food and drink needed for the flight.

The arms push the top part of the van up to the height of the plane, to make loading easier.

This bus carries passengers and aircrew to and from the plane.

Steps for passengers and aircrew

This tug pulls the airliner along when it is on the ground.

The fastest

The first planes and helicopters were slower than today's cars. But, as people learned more about how planes fly and built more powerful engines, planes got faster.

Concorde

Lynx

This is the world's fastest helicopter. It has a top recorded speed of 400km/h (250mph).

Concorde was the fastest airliner ever. Its top speed was over 2,300km/h (1,450mph).
   It was taken out of service in 2003 because it was so expensive to run.

It could travel from New York to London in under three hours.

North American X-15

This plane was flown in the 1960s. It still holds the record as the fastest plane in the world, with a top speed of over 7,200km/h (4,470mph). It had a rocket engine, similar to the ones space rockets use.

Very short wings

Most really fast planes have a pointed nose because it helps the plane punch a hole through the air as it speeds forward.

The plane only had room for a single pilot.

SR-71 Blackbird

The SR-71 first flew in the 1960s and was used until 1998. It was built by the United States as a spy plane. It could fly very high and very fast, which made it hard for other planes to catch.

The SR-71 could fly at over 3,500 km/h (2,170mph).

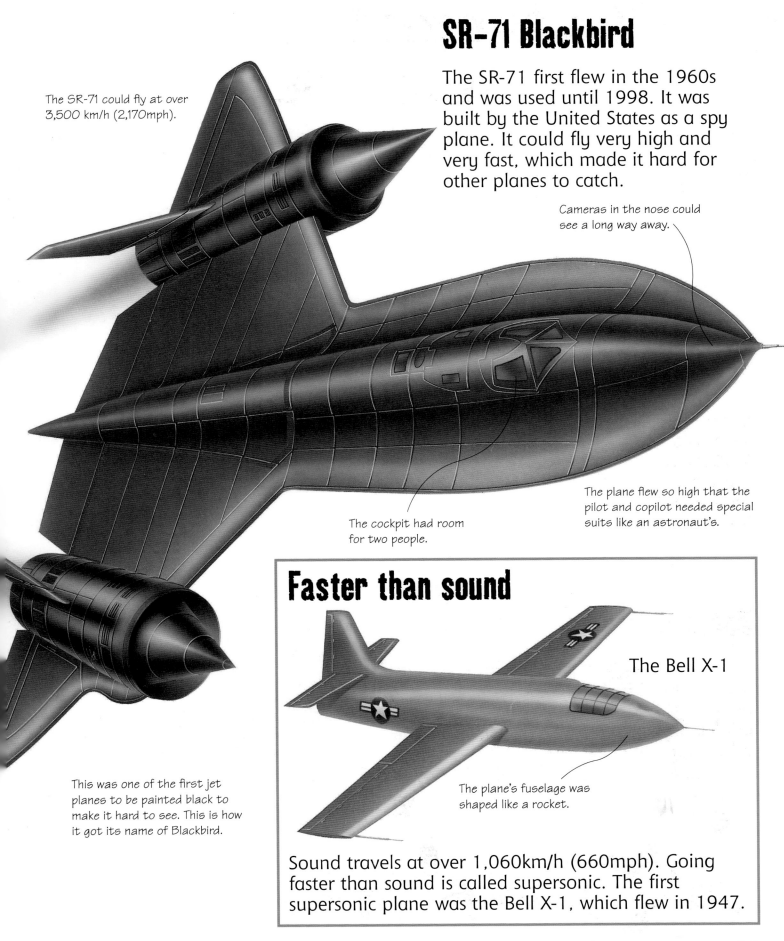

Cameras in the nose could see a long way away.

The cockpit had room for two people.

The plane flew so high that the pilot and copilot needed special suits like an astronaut's.

This was one of the first jet planes to be painted black to make it hard to see. This is how it got its name of Blackbird.

Faster than sound

The Bell X-1

The plane's fuselage was shaped like a rocket.

Sound travels at over 1,060km/h (660mph). Going faster than sound is called supersonic. The first supersonic plane was the Bell X-1, which flew in 1947.

VTOL planes

VTOL stands for Vertical Take Off and Landing. A VTOL plane can fly straight up into the air without needing a runway. It uses powerful blasts of hot air and gases from its engine.

Things called thrusters point the blasts in different directions.

A special machine inside the nose helps guide missiles to their target.

The pilot's right hand moves the control column.

The pilot's left hand controls which way the thrusters point.

The front wheel is called the nosewheel.

The Harrier

The best known VTOL plane is a warplane called the Harrier. There are many different models. This one is a GR7.

The first VTOL plane

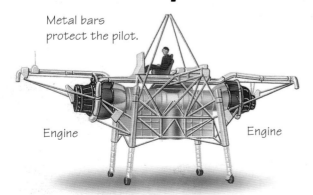

Metal bars protect the pilot.

Engine

Engine

The first ever VTOL plane flew in 1953. It was a test machine and didn't look at all like a normal plane.

Thrusters

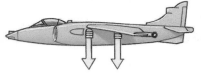

In normal flight, the thrusters point to the back. This pushes the plane forward.

When the thrusters point straight down, the plane can go up and down. It can even hover.

Here, the thrusters are aimed down and slightly forward. The plane can now go backwards.

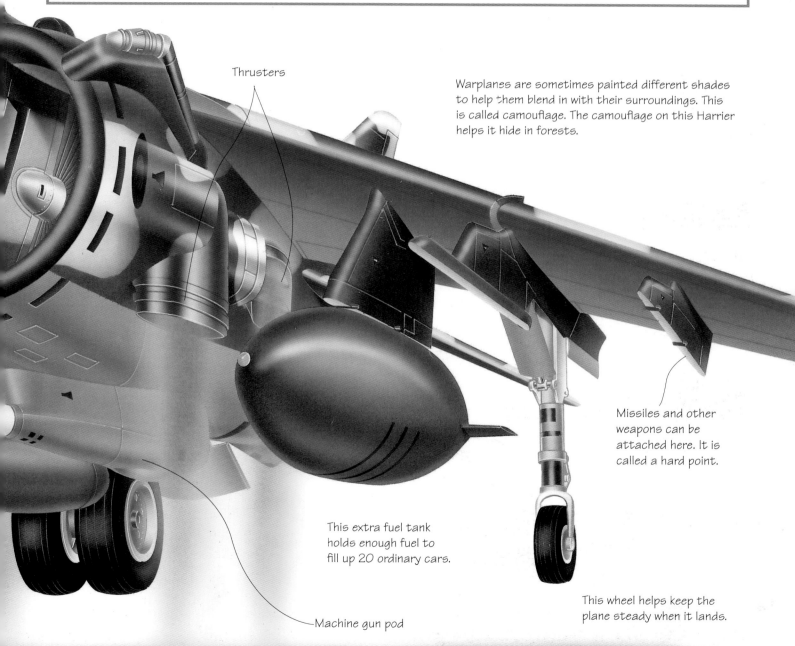

Thrusters

Warplanes are sometimes painted different shades to help them blend in with their surroundings. This is called camouflage. The camouflage on this Harrier helps it hide in forests.

Missiles and other weapons can be attached here. It is called a hard point.

This extra fuel tank holds enough fuel to fill up 20 ordinary cars.

Machine gun pod

This wheel helps keep the plane steady when it lands.

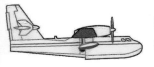

Seaplanes and floatplanes

Most planes need a runway on solid ground. But seaplanes and floatplanes can use water instead. They can take off from and land on water.

Floatplanes

These planes have floats attached to their wings or underneath their bodies. This floatplane is called a De Havilland Beaver. It carries people and mail around countries that have many lakes, such as Canada.

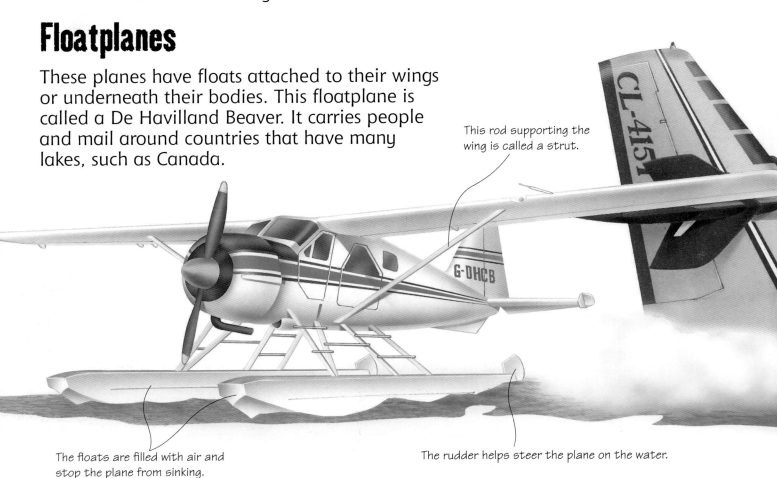

This rod supporting the wing is called a strut.

The floats are filled with air and stop the plane from sinking.

The rudder helps steer the plane on the water.

The largest plane ever

The Spruce Goose was a huge seaplane built in the 1940s, which was paid for by an American millionaire named Howard Hughes. With eight engines and a wingspan the length of a soccer field, it was the largest plane ever made. But it only ever made one flight – a trip of 1.6km (1 mile) in 1947.

Seaplanes

A seaplane's body is called a hull, because it's shaped like a boat and keeps the plane afloat on the water. Seaplanes are sometimes called flying boats.

This seaplane is a Canadair CL-415, which is used to fight forest fires. The plane is brightly painted, so fire fighters on the ground can see it coming and get clear before the plane drops its load of water.

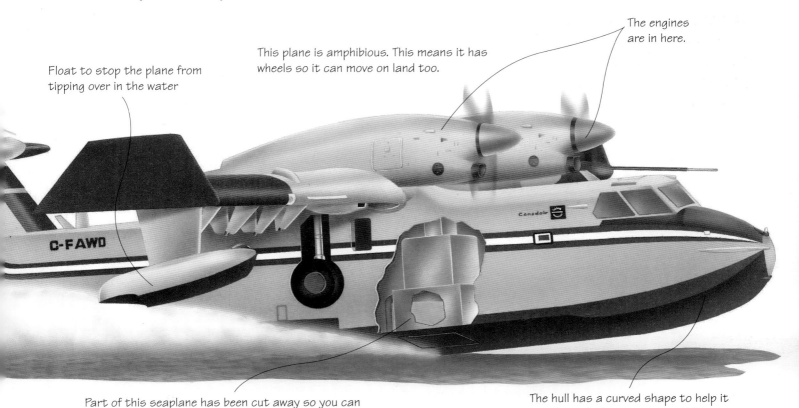

The engines are in here.

This plane is amphibious. This means it has wheels so it can move on land too.

Float to stop the plane from tipping over in the water

C-FAWD

Part of this seaplane has been cut away so you can see the tank that stores water for putting out fires.

The hull has a curved shape to help it run through the water smoothly.

The water bomber

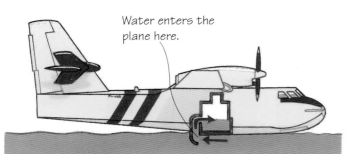

Water enters the plane here.

Hatch opens.

The CL-415 drops water 'bombs' on forest fires to help put them out. The plane collects the water by scooping it up as it skims over lakes or the sea.

In just 10 seconds it can collect enough water to fill 80 baths. It flies back to the fire and dumps all the water out of a big hatch in its body.

Helicopters at work

Helicopters are used for all sorts of jobs, carrying both passengers and cargo. They can fly in places where ordinary planes cannot, so they're often used for rescue work.

Different jobs

Many armed forces use helicopters to transport troops and equipment quickly and in secret.

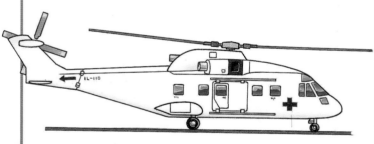

This is an air ambulance used in a big city. It can reach accidents more quickly than an ambulance on the road.

Rotor blades fold back.

Tail folds in half.

This helicopter carries passengers. Its tail and long rotor blades can be folded away to be easily stored.

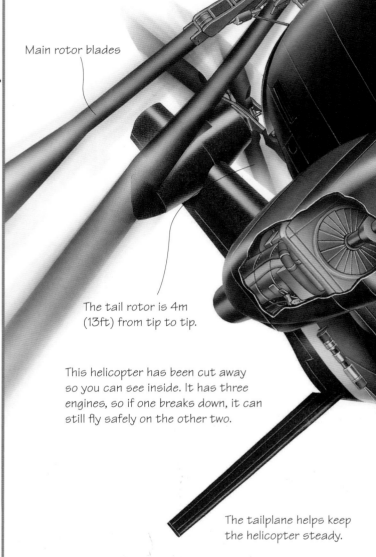

Main rotor blades

The tail rotor is 4m (13ft) from tip to tip.

This helicopter has been cut away so you can see inside. It has three engines, so if one breaks down, it can still fly safely on the other two.

The tailplane helps keep the helicopter steady.

The AW101 can carry 4,000kg (8,700lb) of cargo or 30 passengers.

The AW101

The AW101 was first built in the 1980s and can be used for many different jobs. The one shown here flies over the sea, hunting for enemy ships and submarines.

Wipers keep the windows clear in bad weather.

Radio

This bulge holds special equipment which searches for submarines below the sea's surface.

The helicopter's wheels are kept inside this part called a sponson while it's in the air.

The pilot shown inside the helicopter wears a special suit to protect him from fire.

Aerobatic planes

You can often see planes doing acrobatic moves at airshows, when the pilots make the planes twist and turn in the sky. This is called aerobatics.

Sukhoi Su-26

The Sukhoi Su-26 is a Russian plane that was specially built for aerobatics. It is made from materials which are very light and strong.

The undercarriage is made of a metal called titanium. It is strong but very light.

The gases from the exhaust pipe are mixed with special chemicals to make lots of smoke trails for the crowd to watch.

This plane can roll all the way over in one second.

Aerobatic flying can be very tiring so the pilot must be very fit and strong.

Stunt flying

Some planes do exciting tricks, called stunts, to entertain crowds. One popular stunt is wing walking. The person doesn't actually walk but is strapped tightly to the wing of a flying plane.

Wing walkers sometimes hold flags or wave to crowds.

Wires hold the person in place.

This plane is a Boeing Stearman. It is often used for wing walking.

Sometimes the pilot will do a loop the loop.

Loops and rolls

There are many different moves in aerobatics. The pilot tries to link several moves together.

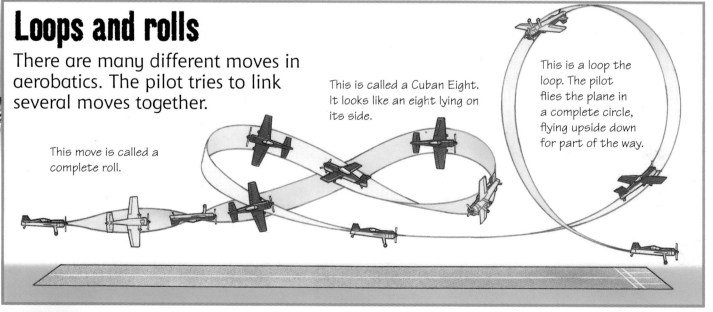

This is called a Cuban Eight. It looks like an eight lying on its side.

This is a loop the loop. The pilot flies the plane in a complete circle, flying upside down for part of the way.

This move is called a complete roll.

 # Formation teams

Military planes often fly in groups for protection and many air forces have special teams, who perform exciting displays at airshows. This is called formation flying.

The Blue Angels

The Blue Angels is a very famous formation team, made up of pilots and planes from the United States Navy.

They first flew in 1946 in planes with propellers. Now they use fast jets called FA-18 Hornets.

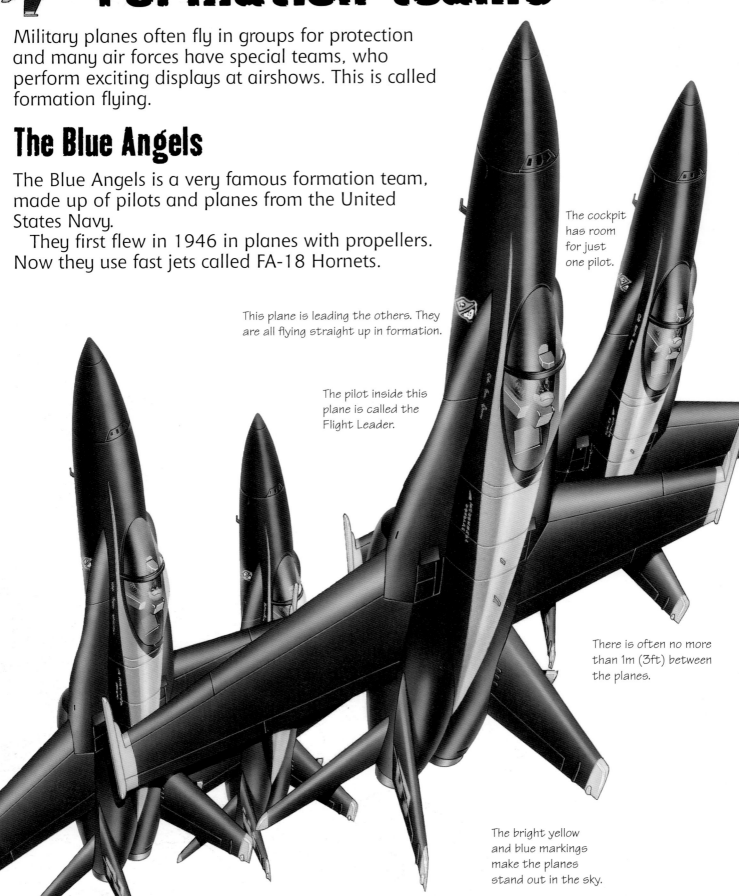

This plane is leading the others. They are all flying straight up in formation.

The cockpit has room for just one pilot.

The pilot inside this plane is called the Flight Leader.

There is often no more than 1m (3ft) between the planes.

The bright yellow and blue markings make the planes stand out in the sky.

Famous formations

Many formations have special names. Here are three used by the British Red Arrows team, which always flies with nine planes.

This is known as a Delta formation.

This is the plane of the Flight Leader.

This is called the Concorde formation because it looks like the Concorde.

This is the diamond formation.

Synchro pair

Some formation teams have a pair of aircraft which split away from the main group, and fly very close to each other. They are called a synchro pair.

The move on the left is called a mirror pair, because these two planes look as if they are reflected in a mirror.

The two planes on the right are flying towards and bypassing each other at high speed. The gap between them is often less than 2m (7½ft).

Giant helicopters

Helicopters come in many sizes. The smallest hold just a pilot and nothing else. The largest can carry lots of people or big machines. The helicopter shown here is a Boeing Chinook.

This helicopter doesn't have a tail rotor to help it turn. Instead, the pilot changes the speed of the two main rotors to move left or right.

The cockpit holds a crew of three.

One of the Chinook's two engines

This searchlight can be used to look for things on the ground at night.

The three crane hooks are for lifting heavy things.

The Boeing Chinook is 30m (100ft) long and can hold 44 passengers.

The Chinook is used by armies to transport soldiers and vehicles. Some airlines also use Chinooks to carry passengers to places that are hard to reach, such as oil rigs.

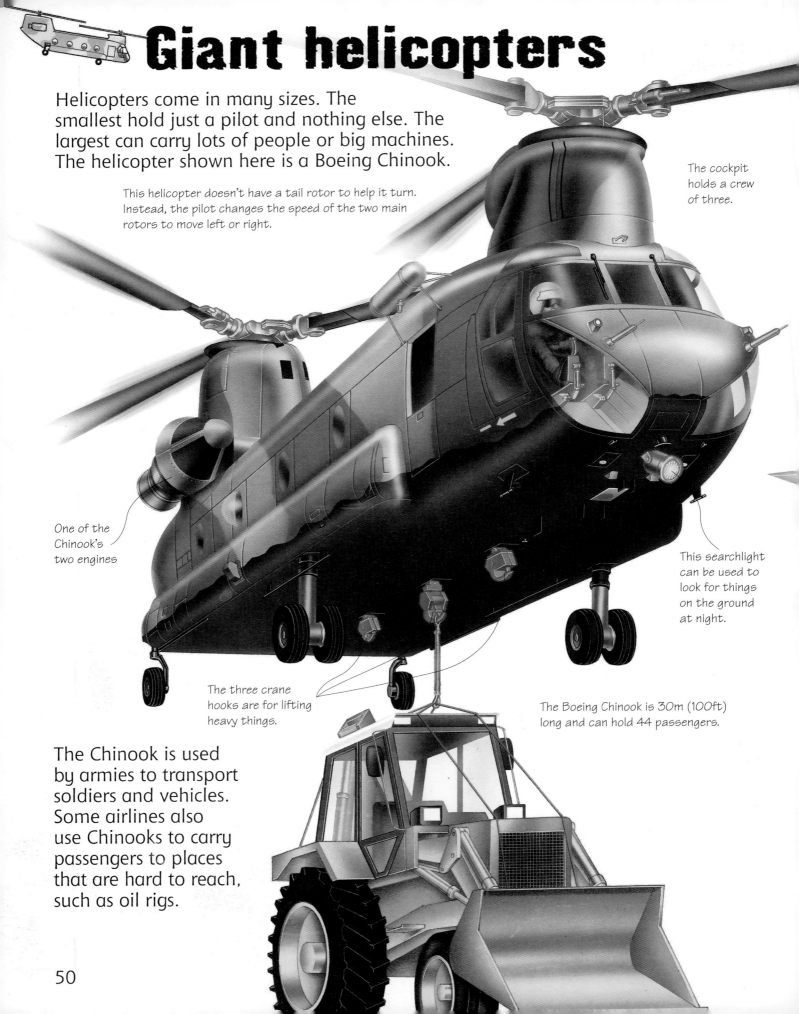

Filling up

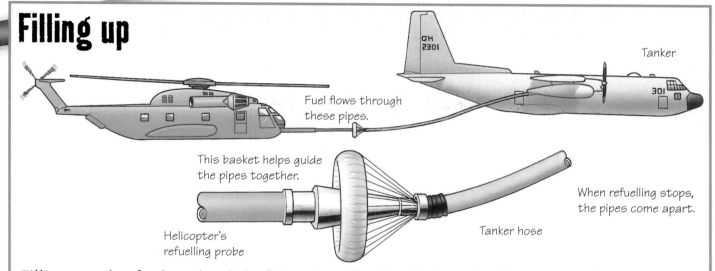

Tanker

Fuel flows through
these pipes.

This basket helps guide
the pipes together.

When refuelling stops,
the pipes come apart.

Helicopter's
refuelling probe

Tanker hose

Filling up the fuel tank while flying is called in-flight refuelling. A tanker plane and helicopter join fuel pipes. Then the tanker pumps fuel out.

Sikorsky Skycrane

The Sikorsky Skycrane is an unusual giant helicopter. It doesn't carry heavy loads inside its body. Instead it flies along with a large container underneath.

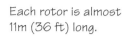

Each rotor is almost
11m (36 ft) long.

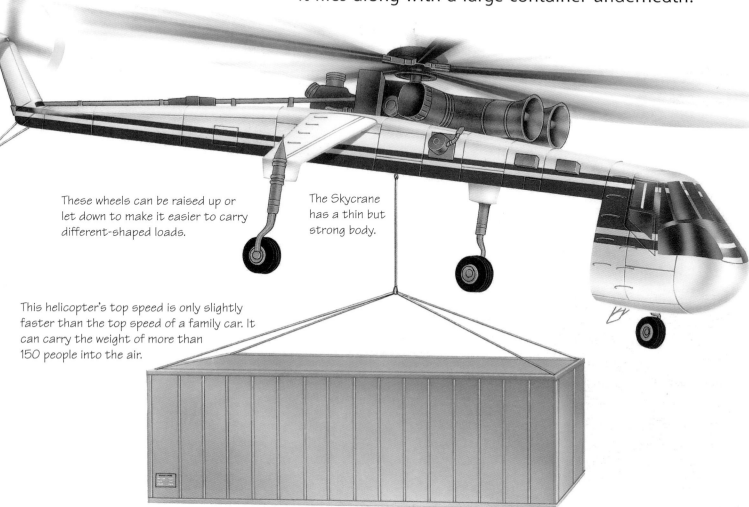

These wheels can be raised up or
let down to make it easier to carry
different-shaped loads.

The Skycrane
has a thin but
strong body.

This helicopter's top speed is only slightly
faster than the top speed of a family car. It
can carry the weight of more than
150 people into the air.

Stealth planes

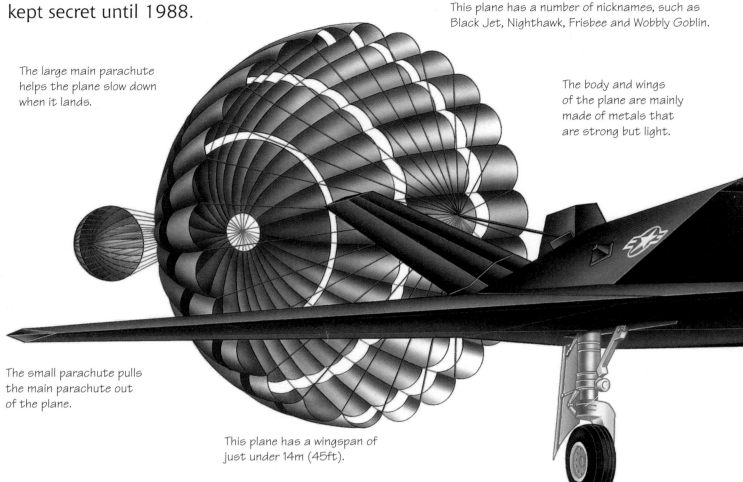

Stealth planes are warplanes that are designed to be difficult to see. This stealth plane is the Lockheed F117A. It first flew in 1981 but was kept secret until 1988.

This plane has a number of nicknames, such as Black Jet, Nighthawk, Frisbee and Wobbly Goblin.

The large main parachute helps the plane slow down when it lands.

The body and wings of the plane are mainly made of metals that are strong but light.

The small parachute pulls the main parachute out of the plane.

This plane has a wingspan of just under 14m (45ft).

How does radar see planes?

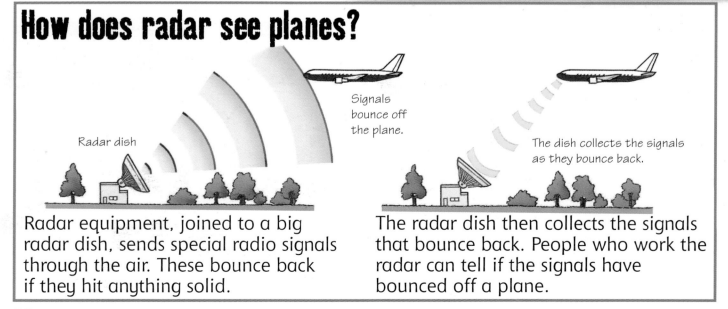

Radar dish

Signals bounce off the plane.

The dish collects the signals as they bounce back.

Radar equipment, joined to a big radar dish, sends special radio signals through the air. These bounce back if they hit anything solid.

The radar dish then collects the signals that bounce back. People who work the radar can tell if the signals have bounced off a plane.

Stealth and the F117A

All the F117A's stealth features help confuse enemies' radar systems. They make the radar think that the plane is not a plane at all, but something else, such as a flock of birds.

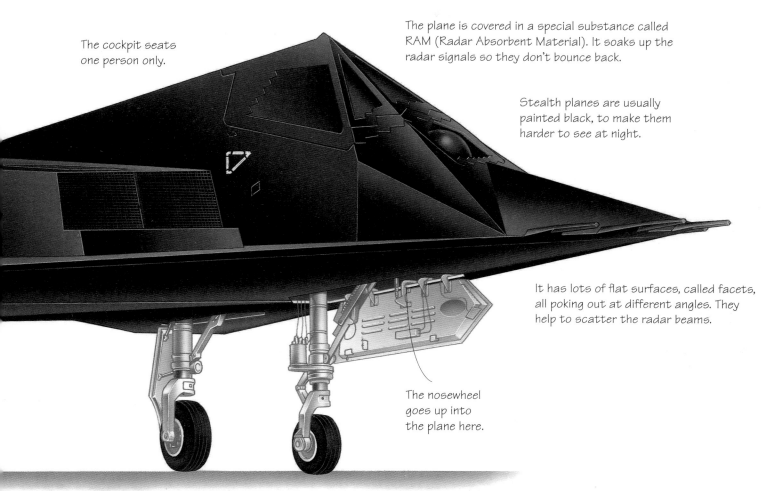

The cockpit seats one person only.

The plane is covered in a special substance called RAM (Radar Absorbent Material). It soaks up the radar signals so they don't bounce back.

Stealth planes are usually painted black, to make them harder to see at night.

It has lots of flat surfaces, called facets, all poking out at different angles. They help to scatter the radar beams.

The nosewheel goes up into the plane here.

Stealth bomber

This is the Northrop B2 bomber. It is made in the United States and first flew in 1989.

It has a very big wingspan of over 52m (170ft).

The B2 has four engines, two on either side of the cockpit.

It can fly 8,000km (5,000 miles) in one trip. That's almost as far as from London to Los Angeles.

The B2 is sometimes called a flying wing, because of its shape.

RACING CARS

Touring car racing

Ever since the first cars were made, people have raced them against each other. There are now many different types of racing.

Touring cars

Touring cars are like ordinary road cars. They don't race on roads, though – they speed around a special racing track.

The centre mirror shows the driver what is happening behind him.

The driver looks in the wing mirror to see if cars are trying to overtake him.

Touring cars can race at speeds up to 275km/h (170mph). When a car goes fast around a bend, two wheels sometimes lift off the ground.

The front of this car has been cut away so you can see inside. As the car races, the engine gets hot. A fan helps cool it down.

Safety clothing

Driving a racing car can be dangerous. Drivers protect themselves by wearing special clothes.

This fireproof balaclava protects the driver's face.

Two shoulder braces protect the driver's head and neck in a crash.

The driver's racing suit is fireproof.

The gloves help stop fire from burning his hands. They are often called gauntlets.

The special boots are very light and fireproof.

Bars inside the car strengthen the car's body.

Touring car races can be very exciting. In most races the cars drive very close to each other.

Crash helmets

Racing drivers must protect their heads in case they crash. A crash helmet stops the head from getting badly hurt.

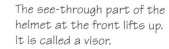

The see-through part of the helmet at the front lifts up. It is called a visor.

57

Grand Prix cars

Grand Prix is one of the most famous types of racing. It is also known as Formula One. The cars race around a track at very high speeds. Some Grand Prix races last for 60 or 70 laps. This is a typical Formula One car.

Wings at the front and back help the car grip the track.

The top speed of a modern Grand Prix car is more than 340km/h (210mph).

A Grand Prix car is made of very light, smooth materials, so it can go as fast as possible.

The very wide back wheels help grip the road and push the car forward at high speed.

This car has been cut away so you can see the engine, which is at the back of the car.

Inside the cockpit

This screen tells the driver how well the car is running.

The driver changes gear using paddles on each side of the steering wheel.

When the driver presses this button, an energy drink is pumped up a tube and into his mouth.

The buttons on the steering wheel adjust different parts of the car as it races around the track.

Map of the race track

Car cam

A tiny camera is fitted to some cars to take exciting pictures of the view from the cockpit. The film is often shown on television. The display at the top shows how long the car has been racing and its speed.

0:55.72 79 MPH

The cockpit is so small, the driver has to remove the steering wheel to get out.

Racing a Grand Prix car can be exhausting, so drivers must be very fit and strong.

The front wheels are narrower than the back wheels. This makes the car easier to steer.

The wheels are used for only one race.

Front wing

Grand Prix cars can weigh less than half a normal family car.

Rallying

Rally cars speed along country tracks and sometimes on roads. They all follow the same route, starting one after the other, and are carefully timed. The car with the fastest time is the winner.

The co-driver's job is to tell the driver what is coming up on the course. He has detailed notes and the driver must completely trust his instructions.

There is a metal frame called a roll cage inside the car to protect the driver and co-driver inside.

Rally cars

Rally cars are similar to ordinary family cars, but much tougher. The cars race over very rough courses with many bumps and dips. It can be very dangerous, so the cars needs to be extra strong.

These wheels are specially made to grip the rough tracks.

Inside the rally car

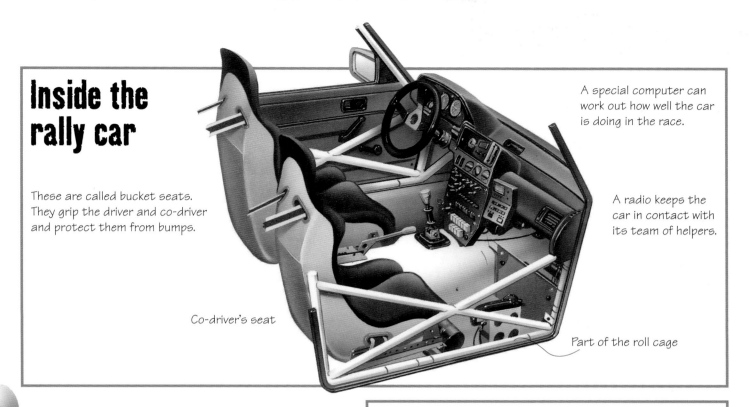

These are called bucket seats. They grip the driver and co-driver and protect them from bumps.

A special computer can work out how well the car is doing in the race.

A radio keeps the car in contact with its team of helpers.

Co-driver's seat

Part of the roll cage

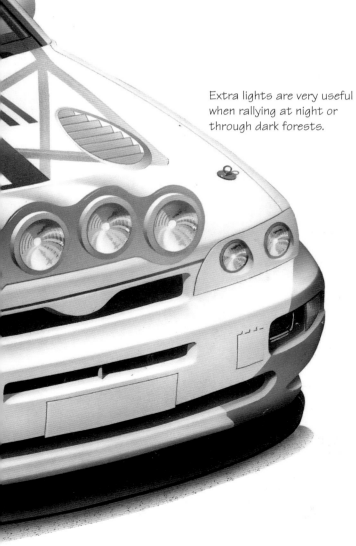

Extra lights are very useful when rallying at night or through dark forests.

The rally

Rallies are made up of lots of different parts, or stages. These test the car and driver in different ways.

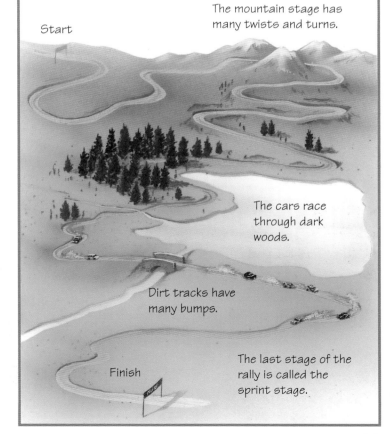

Start

The mountain stage has many twists and turns.

The cars race through dark woods.

Dirt tracks have many bumps.

Finish

The last stage of the rally is called the sprint stage.

Le Mans cars

One of the most famous races in the world is held at a race track in Le Mans in France. It lasts for 24 hours and the winner is the car that does the most laps in that time.

This car is a Porsche 962. It has a top speed of 400km/h (250mph).

Le Mans cars are driven by teams of drivers. When one driver gets tired, another takes over.

The winning car will run at an average speed of over 210km/h (130mph) for the whole 24 hours.

PORSCHE

Shell

BOSCH

OXIDIZING AGENT

5

DUNLOP

Shell

11

11

DUNLOP

BOSCH

This car's engine is eight times as powerful as the engine of an ordinary family car.

The body's shape lets the air flow over it easily so the car can go faster.

Old Le Mans cars

Cars have been racing at Le Mans since 1923. Cars made by Bentley, Ferrari, Ford, Jaguar and Mercedes have all won there.

This Bentley Speed Six won Le Mans in 1929 and 1930.

There is a spare wheel attached to the side of the car.

Porsche 911 Turbo

The Porsche 911 Turbo is one
of the most famous Le Mans cars.

This car can go from standing
still to 100 km/h (60mph) in
under six seconds.

The Porsche 911 first raced at
Le Mans in the 1960s. Modern
911s still race there today.

Strong headlights are very
important, as the car races all night.

Quick repairs

The back part lifts off to show
the engine and gearbox.

The front part lifts off to show
the front lights and wheels.

This car is a
Jaguar XJ220C.

During the race, Le Mans cars often stop at the side of the track in areas known as
the pits. Parts of the car's body lift off in sections so repairs can be made quickly.

Indycars

Indycars look a lot like Grand Prix cars but they're bigger and heavier.

They race in Canada and Australia, as well as the United States. They're named after the Indianapolis 500, a famous race held in the city of Indianapolis in the United States.

An air scoop forces air onto the brakes to keep them cool.

Wings

Some Indycars have wings, like planes. When air passes over a plane wing, it lifts the plane up.

Plane wing rises up.

Air

In Indycars, the wings are turned upside down. When air passes over the wing, the car is pushed down onto the track.

Wing pushes car down.

Air

The car grips the track.

Indycars and Grand Prix cars have two of these wings, one at the back and one at the front.

Rear wing

Front wing

Rods called suspension arms hold the wheel firmly in position.

Front wing

The Indycar's smooth body helps it go as fast as possible.

Changing wheels

When the track is dry, smooth wheels called slicks are used. They let the car go very fast.

In wet weather, grooved wheels are used, as they grip the slippery track.

Wet weather wheels

Slick wheels

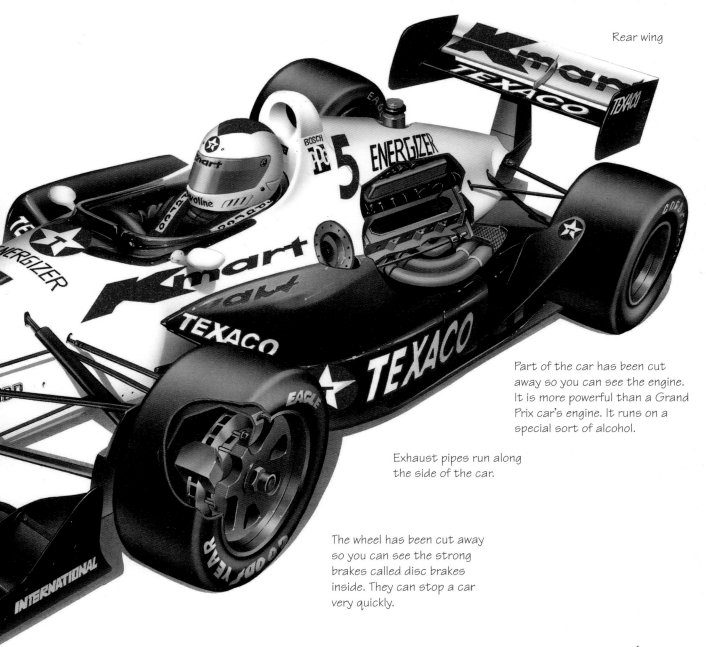

Rear wing

Part of the car has been cut away so you can see the engine. It is more powerful than a Grand Prix car's engine. It runs on a special sort of alcohol.

Exhaust pipes run along the side of the car.

The wheel has been cut away so you can see the strong brakes called disc brakes inside. They can stop a car very quickly.

Races and tracks

Indycar races are often called '500s', because they are 500 miles (805km) long. They sometimes use the same tracks as NASCAR racing (see page 72).

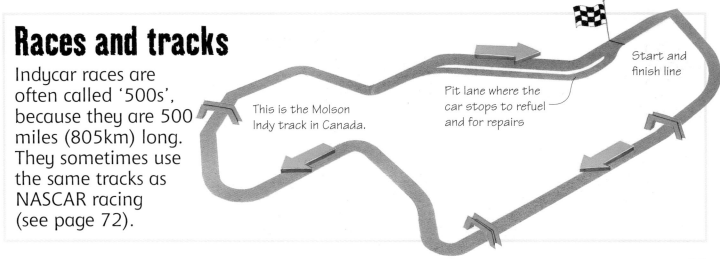

This is the Molson Indy track in Canada.

Pit lane where the car stops to refuel and for repairs

Start and finish line

Desert rallying

Rallies are held all over the world. Some of the toughest rallies are through deserts, such as the Sahara in North Africa. Desert rallies include steep sand dunes and hard, rocky ground.

This is called an air intake. It allows air into the engine, which is in the back of the car.

Wipers keep sand off the windshield.

This is a French car called a Citroën ZX.

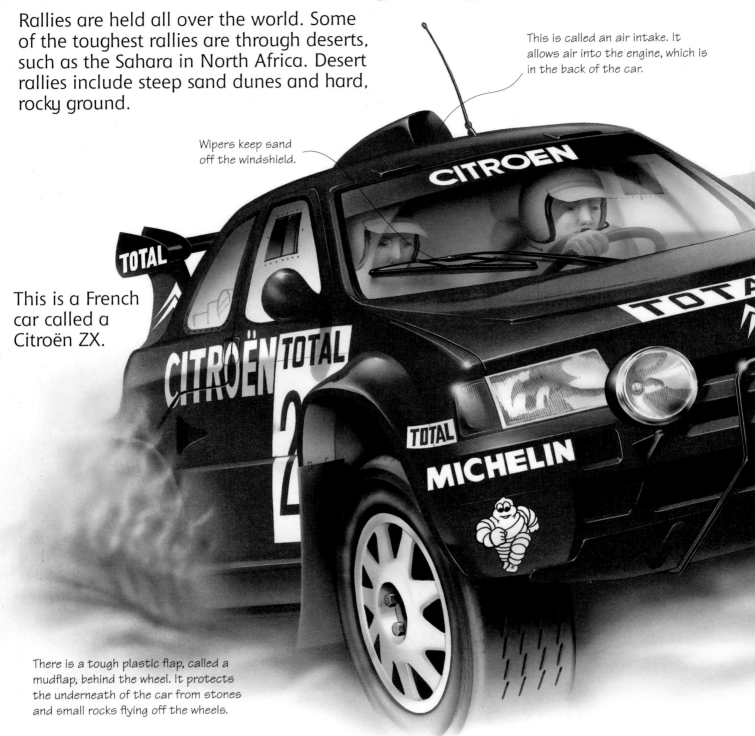

There is a tough plastic flap, called a mudflap, behind the wheel. It protects the underneath of the car from stones and small rocks flying off the wheels.

There are no fuel stations in the desert, so this car carries over five times as much fuel as a normal car.

The cars often break down. They have to be repaired on the way by the support team.

The support team

A desert rally team includes many vehicles other than the actual rally car.

The car carries a few spare parts, supplies and lots of water.

Extra lights are used for rallying at night.

Some big rally teams use a helicopter. It can spot any problems ahead of the rally car.

This canteen van makes meals for all the members of the rally team.

The rally team's medical van has space inside for up to four patients.

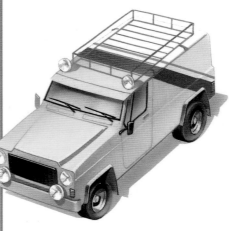

A sheet of tiny wire loops at the front, called a net cover, lets air in to cool the car but keeps stones out.

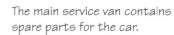

The main service van contains spare parts for the car.

This motorcycle can pick up the drivers or pass messages to them if the radio breaks down.

Monster trucks

These amazing cars are pick-up trucks with special features added. The trucks are raised high off the ground so that they can drive over things in their way.

They race in pairs, speeding over bumpy and muddy courses.

In ordinary cars, power from the engine goes either to the back or front set of wheels. In monster trucks, it goes to both. This is called four-wheel drive.

Many parts of the truck are covered in chrome, a bright, shiny metal.

These are shock absorbers. They act like cushions as the car goes over bumps.

These wheels come from massive farm vehicles.

Old, wrecked cars are put in the monster racer's way.

Monster crawler

This monster truck has crawler tracks, like a tank or a bulldozer, instead of wheels.

One wheel and tyre alone weighs 440kg (1000lbs).

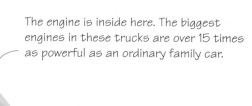

The engine is inside here. The biggest engines in these trucks are over 15 times as powerful as an ordinary family car.

How high is a monster racer?

Monster racers are twice as high as an ordinary pick-up truck. They are over 3.5m (11ft) high.

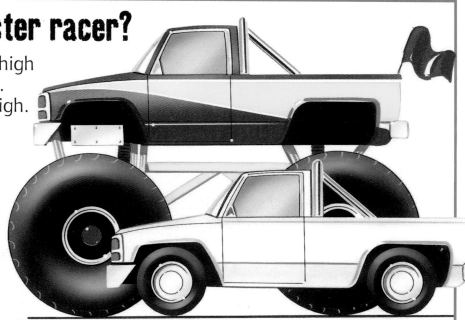

The wheel arch is designed for a normal-sized wheel.

Each huge wheel is larger than a tall person.

Dirt track racers

Dirt track racers race around oval tracks made of dirt. Up to four of them race against each other at once. The big car you can see here is from the United States.

European stock cars

These cars are like the American dirt track racers, but smaller. They use many parts from ordinary cars and are much cheaper to build.

A large crash bar in front protects the car when it bumps into the other cars.

Plates on the sides of the roof push the air away. This helps to keep the car upright as it goes around corners.

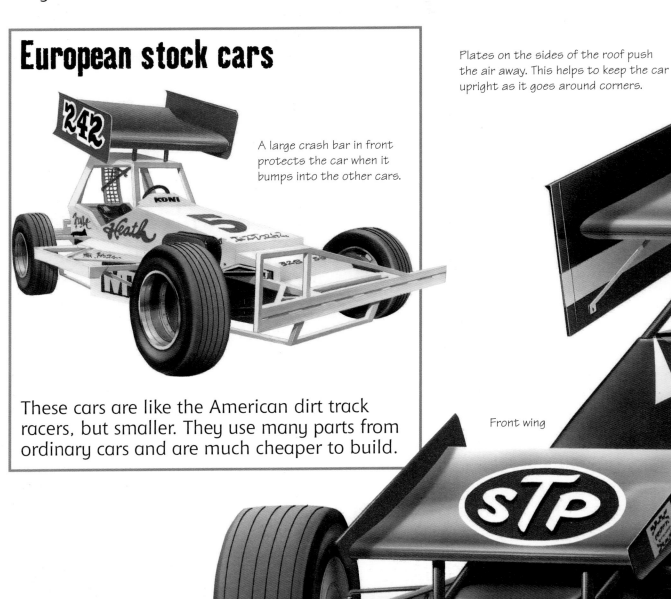

Front wing

The grooves on a wheel are called tread. Different treads are needed for different types of ground. Dirt track cars use a very deep tread.

The front axle joins the two front wheels together.

Names of companies who helped build or pay for the car are shown here.

A roll cage protects the driver.

The driver wears a set of straps called a racing harness.

The back wheels are very wide. This helps the driver control the car around corners.

Turning corners

Turning corners as fast as possible is one of the most difficult parts of racing. Drivers must react quickly if anything goes wrong.

The driver steers around the corner.

If the car is going too fast when it turns, the back wheels may swing out to the side.

The driver must slide the back wheels to the other side, to make the car point the right way again.

 # NASCAR racing

NASCAR is a very popular type of racing in the United States. The cars race around the track at speeds of over 320km/h (200mph).

They all go at about the same speed, so the races are very close and exciting. The cars often finish with a lot of bumps and dents.

Bars strengthen the windshield and roof.

Air goes in through a hole at the front to cool the engine.

Parts of this car have been cut away so you can see the engine and the metal bars that protect it.

NASCAR tracks

Most NASCAR tracks are called ovals. The cars race around the track and enter the pits for fuel and repairs.

Spectators sit in rows of seats all around the edge of the track. These are called the grandstands.

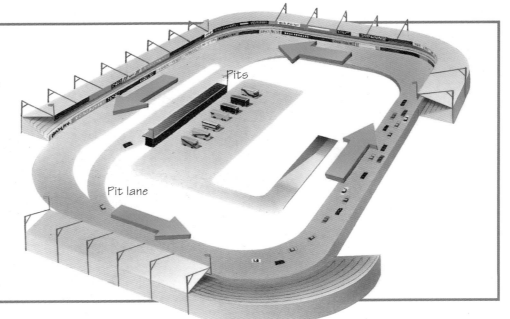

Pits

Pit lane

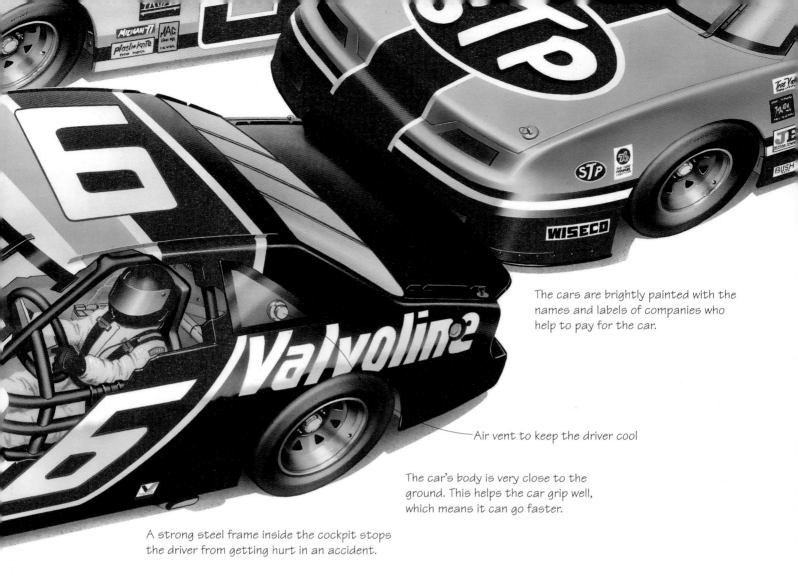

The cars are brightly painted with the names and labels of companies who help to pay for the car.

Air vent to keep the driver cool

The car's body is very close to the ground. This helps the car grip well, which means it can go faster.

A strong steel frame inside the cockpit stops the driver from getting hurt in an accident.

Banked track

NASCAR tracks have wide corners on a slope, known as banked curves. Most of the bumps and crashes happen here.

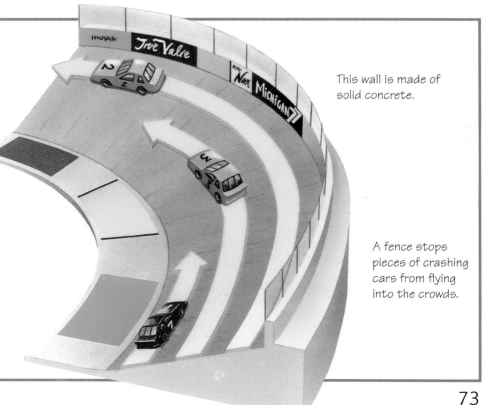

This wall is made of solid concrete.

A fence stops pieces of crashing cars from flying into the crowds.

Drivers can choose to go around corners at a high, medium or low level.

Dragsters

Dragsters are cars that race a short distance along a straight track. They race in pairs against each other.

The car needs a fast start so the engine is warmed up before the race.

Dragsters spin their back wheels just before a race. This is called burning out. It creates a lot of smoke.

Wheelie bars

A wheelie is when the front of a car lifts up into the air, slowing the cars down. Some dragsters have a wheelie bar at the back to stop this from happening.

Wheel

Wheelie bar

The wheelie bar stops the car from lifting up too much.

Burning out makes the wheels hot and sticky. This helps the car grip the track.

The front wheels are much smaller than the back wheels.

The drag strip

The track that these cars race along is called a drag strip.

The strip is flat and straight, and only 400m (¼ mile) long.

The cars burn out and then move to the start line to wait for the green light.

Then the cars start racing. The race only lasts for five or six seconds.

The big box in front forces air into the engine. It is called an air scoop.

The cars line up on either side of the starting lights, which are known as the Christmas tree.

The lights come on to tell the drivers to get ready.

When the light turns green, the cars start racing.

The body is very light so the car can go even faster.

Most dragsters use a special mixture of chemicals called nitro-methanol as fuel.

The cars must drive straight. They are kept apart by a concrete barrier.

Cars like these reach speeds as high as 320km/h (190mph).

The cars sometimes use a parachute to slow down once the race is over.

Learning to race

Racing is quite different from ordinary driving. Most people who want to race train at special schools.

Karting

Karts are the smallest cars used for racing, and most drivers learn to race in them first.

Basic karts can reach speeds of around 100km/h (60mph), so the drivers have to wear crash helmets.

The engine on this kart is 10 times smaller than the engine in an ordinary family car.

Basic karts have no gears, just an accelerator and a brake.

 ## Saloon car

When you first learn to drive on a track, an instructor sits beside you. The instructor drives first, to show you the best way around the track.

A roll cage inside the car protects the driver and the instructor.

If the car turns too fast, a wheel lifts off the track.

Learner racing driver

Instructor

Off-road racing

Racing across countryside where there is no track is called off-road racing.
It teaches you to drive over muddy, bumpy and slippery ground.
This is good practice for many other types of racing.

Crash bars protect
the front of the car.

Chunky wheels help the car
to drive through deep mud.

Flaps behind the wheels stop mud from
flying off and onto the windows.

Single-seater racing

After lots of races in karts, a
driver can try out a single-seater
car. This is the first step to driving
a real Grand Prix car.

A metal hoop behind the
seat helps protect the driver
if the car rolls over.

These cars can reach half the speed
of a top Grand Prix racing car.

TRACTORS

Tractors

Tractors do many different jobs on a farm and work in all sorts of weather.
Farmers drive them over bumpy, muddy fields, so they have to be tough and hard-wearing.

Cab where the driver sits

The front of the tractor has been cut away, so you can see the engine. It must be very powerful so it can pull heavy loads.

Tractors can go on roads but they cannot move as fast as cars or trucks.

Headlights

The main part of the tractor is called the chassis.

A weight block at the front helps the front wheels grip the ground when there is a heavy machine at the back.

Tough, thick wheels

When the tractor drives on roads, this flashing light warns other drivers to slow down.

Tractors can tip right over if they drive up very steep slopes. There is a metal frame to protect the farmer if that happens.

Tractors can turn around in small spaces. This helps them avoid squashing crops in the fields.

Mud and bumps

The deep grooves in tractor wheels grip wet, muddy ground.

A tractor's body is high up to stop it from getting damaged by bumpy ground.

Its powerful engine keeps the tractor going up steep ground.

Pulling tools

Tractors pull many different farming tools behind them.

The tools are fixed to three metal links behind the cab. A metal pole called a Power Take-Off (PTO) carries power from the tractor's engine to the tools to make them work.

PTO

Tractors at work

Farmers use tractors to prepare the ground for growing crops. Different tools are fixed behind the tractor and driven up and down the fields.

Plough

Ploughs break up and turn over hard, flat earth, and bury weeds. This makes the ground better for planting seeds in.

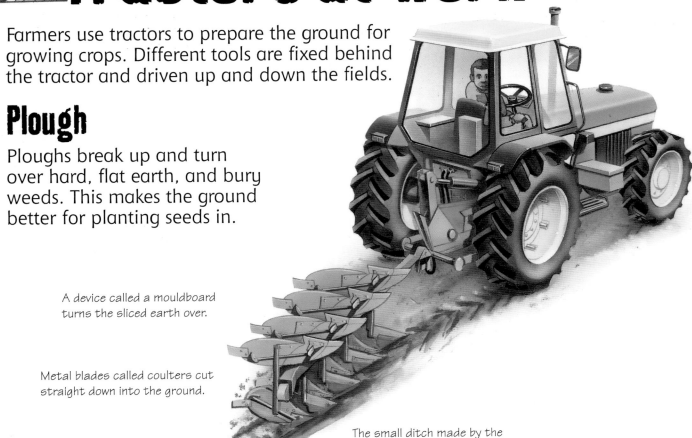

A device called a mouldboard turns the sliced earth over.

Metal blades called coulters cut straight down into the ground.

The small ditch made by the blades is called a furrow.

Harrow

This tractor is pulling a part called a disc-harrow.
Harrowing breaks down the big slices of earth the plough has made.

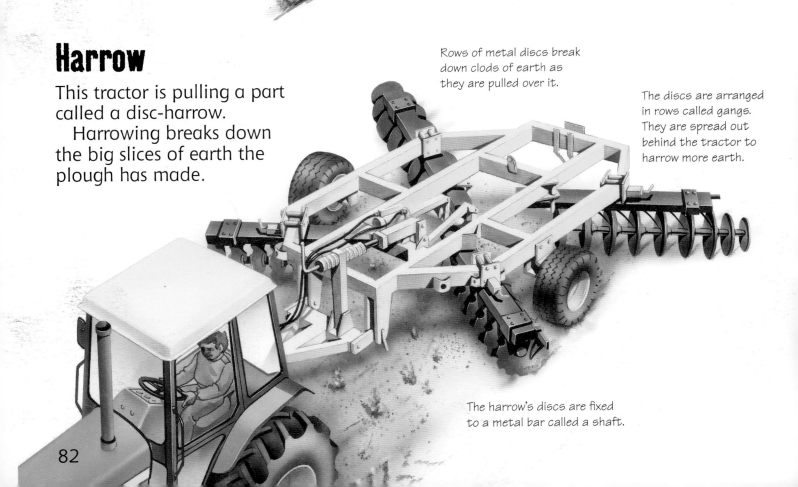

Rows of metal discs break down clods of earth as they are pulled over it.

The discs are arranged in rows called gangs. They are spread out behind the tractor to harrow more earth.

The harrow's discs are fixed to a metal bar called a shaft.

Roller

The roller smooths the earth after harrowing. It makes the field level for planting seeds in.

Each roller is made up of 20 steel rings.

A tractor can roll a field more quickly with wide rollers because it has to make fewer trips up and down it.

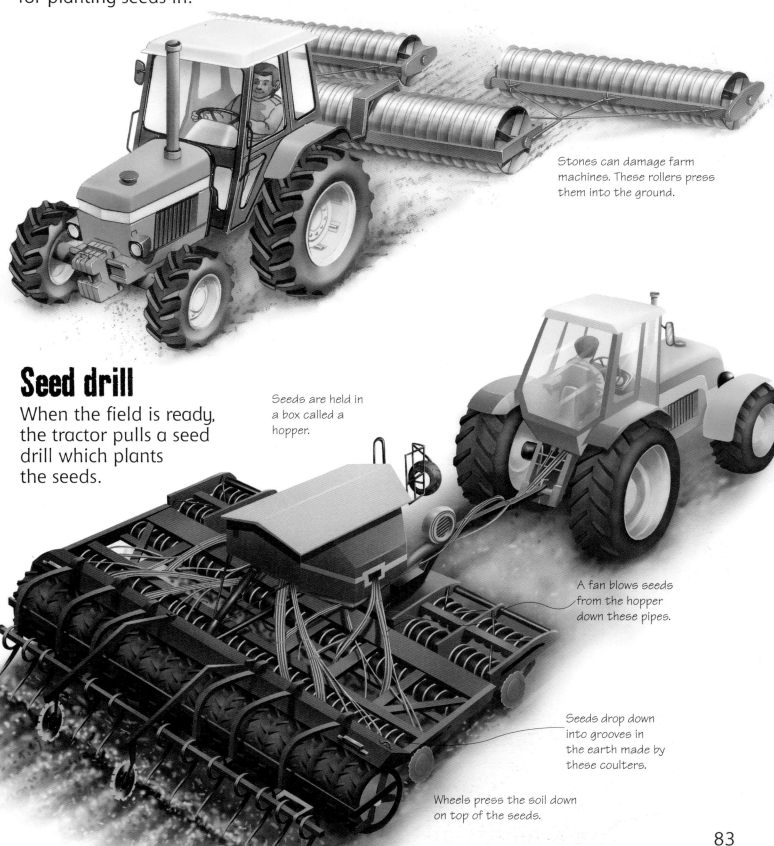

Stones can damage farm machines. These rollers press them into the ground.

Seed drill

When the field is ready, the tractor pulls a seed drill which plants the seeds.

Seeds are held in a box called a hopper.

A fan blows seeds from the hopper down these pipes.

Seeds drop down into grooves in the earth made by these coulters.

Wheels press the soil down on top of the seeds.

Spreaders and sprayers

Crops need food called fertilizer to grow well, and they may need protection from insects and diseases, too. Here are some machines that spread fertilizer over fields and spray them with pest-killing chemicals.

Muckspreader

Farm animals make a lot of muck, called manure or dung, which is a very good fertilizer. A tractor pulls a machine called a muckspreader over the fields to scatter manure over crops.

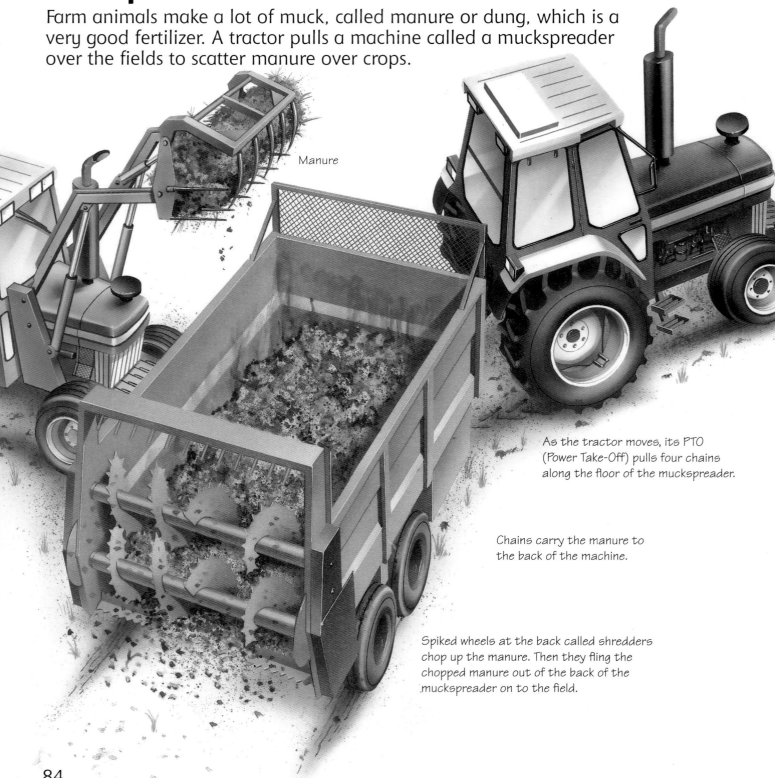

Manure

As the tractor moves, its PTO (Power Take-Off) pulls four chains along the floor of the muckspreader.

Chains carry the manure to the back of the machine.

Spiked wheels at the back called shredders chop up the manure. Then they fling the chopped manure out of the back of the muckspreader on to the field.

Sprayer

Some farmers spray fields with chemicals called pesticides to kill insects and diseases. Pesticides can be poisonous, so farmers have to use them very carefully.

As the tractor moves along, the sprayer fixed to it sprays out exactly the right amount of pesticide.

Super sprayers

If a field is very big, some farmers fix extra wide sprayers behind their tractors, to spray their land as quickly as possible. This sprayer is about as long as two buses.

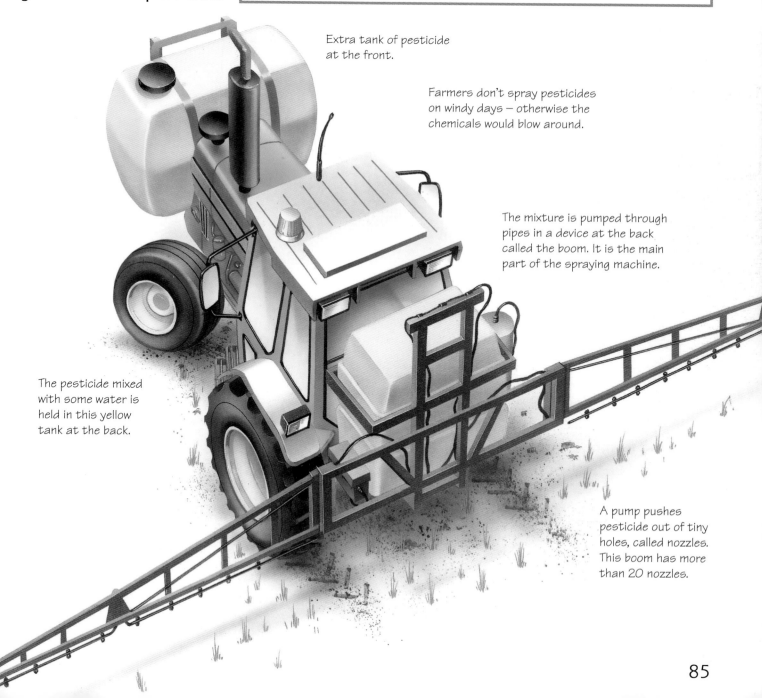

Extra tank of pesticide at the front.

Farmers don't spray pesticides on windy days – otherwise the chemicals would blow around.

The mixture is pumped through pipes in a device at the back called the boom. It is the main part of the spraying machine.

The pesticide mixed with some water is held in this yellow tank at the back.

A pump pushes pesticide out of tiny holes, called nozzles. This boom has more than 20 nozzles.

Combine harvester

A machine called a combine harvester is used for crops such as wheat, peas and barley, which are made up of stalks with grains at the top.

The combine harvester does two jobs at the same time. First, it cuts and gathers up, or harvests, the crops. Then it separates the grains from their stalks. This is called threshing.

Sorting out

A combine cuts and pulls in the crop.

Inside the cab

Some combine harvesters have computers in the cab. They tell the driver how full the grain tank is and how well the machine is working.

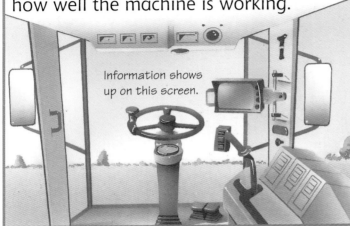

Information shows up on this screen.

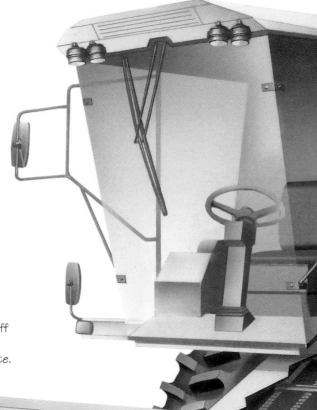

Parts of this combine harvester have been cut away so you can see the machinery inside.

A blade cuts the stalks off at the bottom. It makes about 1,000 cuts a minute.

This wheel, called a reel, spins around. It is covered with metal spikes called tines.

The tines push the cut stalks into the combine harvester.

Inside the machine, a stone trap catches any stones.

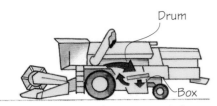

Drum

Box

A spinning drum inside shakes the grains off the stalks. They collect in a box.

Straw

Chaff

The stalks are pushed out as straw. Fans blow out waste called chaff.

Trailer

The grain is unloaded into a trailer. A tractor pulls it to a dry barn to be stored.

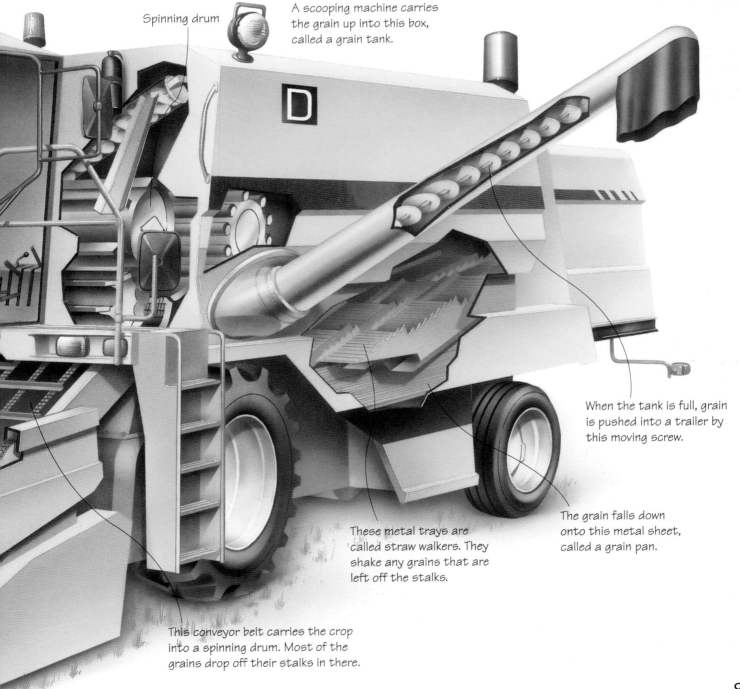

Spinning drum

A scooping machine carries the grain up into this box, called a grain tank.

When the tank is full, grain is pushed into a trailer by this moving screw.

These metal trays are called straw walkers. They shake any grains that are left off the stalks.

The grain falls down onto this metal sheet, called a grain pan.

This conveyor belt carries the crop into a spinning drum. Most of the grains drop off their stalks in there.

Hay and straw

Farmers use these machines to cut and gather dried grass, such as hay and straw. Hay is nutritious, and is used to feed farm animals. Straw is used for their bedding.

Mower

This tractor is pulling a grass mower. It cuts grass and leaves it in rows called swaths on the field.

Power from the tractor's PTO goes through this metal arm to make the blades turn.

These blades spin around about 3,000 times in a minute.

Swath

Swath turner

Straw and grass must be completely dry before it's made into bundles called bales. The swath turner helps dry out swaths by turning them over.

These are swath boards. They can move in or out to make thinner or fatter swaths.

These are called finger wheels. They pick up grass in the swath and turn it over.

Baler

Wrapping hay and straw into bales makes it easier to carry them around. A machine called a round baler is used to make round bales.

How it works

Drum

Bale

Metal fingers at the front push hay and straw into the baler. Spinning drums roll them into a bale.

String ties the bale up tight. Then the top half of the baler opens. The new bale falls into the field.

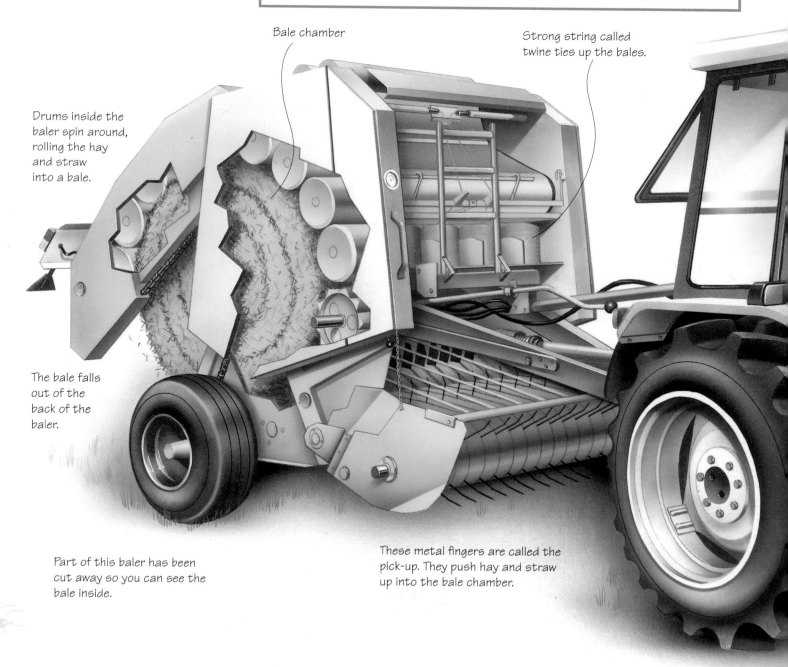

Bale chamber

Strong string called twine ties up the bales.

Drums inside the baler spin around, rolling the hay and straw into a bale.

The bale falls out of the back of the baler.

Part of this baler has been cut away so you can see the bale inside.

These metal fingers are called the pick-up. They push hay and straw up into the bale chamber.

Lifters and loaders

Farmers fix tools to the front of tractors too. These tools are specially built to lift different loads and carry them around the farm.

Grab

A grab is fixed to a tractor to pick up and move silage or manure.

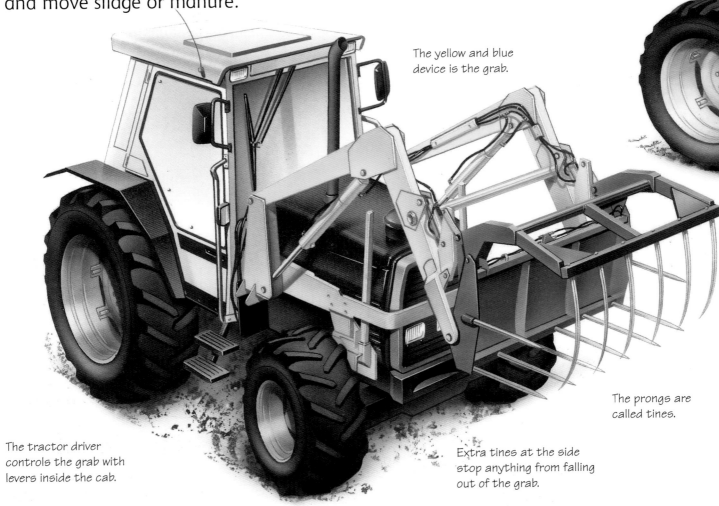

The yellow and blue device is the grab.

The prongs are called tines.

The tractor driver controls the grab with levers inside the cab.

Extra tines at the side stop anything from falling out of the grab.

How the grab works

The driver pulls a lever to open up the tines like a mouth.

Another lever makes the tines close around the manure. The grab lifts up.

The tines open to let the manure fall out where the driver wants to unload it.

Bale fork

Bales of hay and straw are difficult to move by hand. Farmers fix a bale fork to their tractors to move them around the farm.

This smaller spike stops the bale from swaying from side to side as the tractor drives along.

This spike sticks deep into the bale.

This metal pedal pushes the bale off the spikes.

Farmers can pick up mud, stones, manure or grain in the loader bucket.

A weight on the back of the tractor stops it from falling forwards when it carries heavy loads. It is called the counterweight.

Control lever

The boom bends in the middle to help the bucket scoop things up.

Tractor loader

The tractor loader has a bucket fixed in front of the cab for scooping things into.

The farmer can take the loader bucket off the tractor in only a few minutes.

Around the farm

Tractors do many unusual jobs on a farm. The farmer can fix all sorts of tools to the tractor for different tasks.

Ditch digger

If a field stays too wet after rain, crops won't be able to grow in it. So the farmer has to drain the water from the field.

This tractor is using a backhoe to dig drainage ditches. The water will flow off the field and into the ditches.

Hedge-trimmer

This tractor has an arm called a hedge-trimmer fixed to it. As the tractor moves, the trimmer's metal blades cut the tops off hedges.

The farmer faces backwards so he can see where he is digging and work the controls.

The digging arm can move up and down or from side to side.

Metal legs stop the tractor from toppling over as it digs.

The backhoe is fixed to the back of the tractor by this frame.

Post driver

Tractors can help the farmer put fences around the fields. This tractor has a tool called a post driver fixed to it. It pushes fence posts into the ground, and the farmer joins them up with wire.

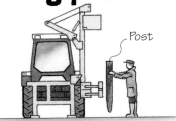

The farmer slides a wooden post into a slot in the post driver.

He puts the post driver above the place where he wants a fence post.

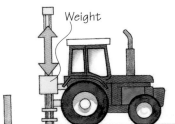

Heavy weights slide down the driver and bang the post into the ground.

The metal frame of the post driver is very strong.

This heavy weight hammers the posts into the ground.

Some frames can swing around to work on either side of the tractor.

This post driver can bash in a post every 40 seconds.

Post

Post drivers are sometimes called post bashers.

Metal legs called stabilizers hold the tractor steady as it thumps in posts.

93

Giant tractor

Ordinary tractors are not powerful enough for some farming jobs so huge machines like this one do them instead. This tractor usually works in the big wheat fields of North America. It can work for about 24 hours without stopping.

Wheels and weight

Giant tractors like this are very heavy. They need eight wheels to carry their enormous weight.

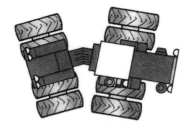

All eight wheels turn together to make the huge tractor move and turn around.

The tractor's wheels are very wide. This helps them grip more ground to pull the tractor along.

Giant tractors like this are heavy and slow. They can only go about as fast as a bicycle, but their engines are much more powerful than ordinary tractor engines.

Headlights

Big Bud

Big Bud is one of the biggest tractors in the world. Its wheels are taller than a man.

Big Bud was specially built to work on big farms in North America.

The eight wide wheels spread out the tractor's weight over more ground, stopping it from sinking into the field.

The air filter stops dust from getting into the engine and damaging it.

Sitting in this cab is like looking out of an upstairs window of a house.

Thick glass stops too much engine noise from getting into the cab.

Giant tractors often work at night, too. They have lights at the front and at the back.

Some of the wheat fields in North America are so long that it can take an hour to drive from one end to the other.

Root crop machines

Farmers use root crop machines to plant and harvest vegetables that grow under the ground, such as potatoes and carrots.

Potato planter

This machine plants small potatoes, called seed potatoes, under the ground as it moves.

The hopper can hold 30 sacks of seed potatoes.

The seed potatoes fall into grooves called furrows in the field.

These red metal blades cover the seed potatoes with earth.

Root crop harvester

This machine gathers the root crops when they have grown.

Chains drag over the earth to make nicely shaped ridges.

Blades called shares slice under the potatoes and lift the whole plant out of the ground.

Inside the machine

The root crop harvester lifts the vegetables out of the ground.

It shakes the earth off them and passes their leaves out of the back.

Moving belts carry the vegetables up past the pickers into a trailer.

Machines like this harvest carrots and onions, as well.

Pickers pick out any stones and bad potatoes as they pass by.

The elevator carries the potatoes up to the pickers as the harvester moves forwards.

A conveyor belt called a web carries the potatoes up inside the harvester.

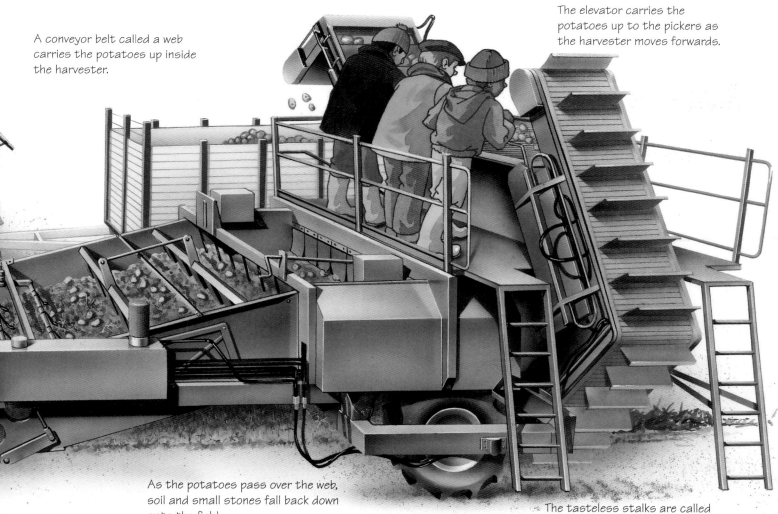

As the potatoes pass over the web, soil and small stones fall back down onto the field.

The tasteless stalks are called haulm. They are pushed out of the back of the harvesting machine.

Crawler tractor

A crawler tractor has rubber crawler tracks instead of normal wheels. Farmers use crawler tracks in wet, muddy fields where ordinary tractors might get stuck. They can also pull heavy loads without their tracks slipping or sinking.

Inside the cab

Door

Clutch

Brake

Control levers

The seat can turn around to face either side.

The cab can be made cooler or warmer, and there are cushions to move into the most comfortable position.

Farmers work long hours, so the cab is designed to be as comfortable as possible. All the controls must be easy to use and easy to reach.

Guide blocks stop the crawler tracks from slipping off as the tractor moves.

Steel cables inside the rubber track make it stronger.

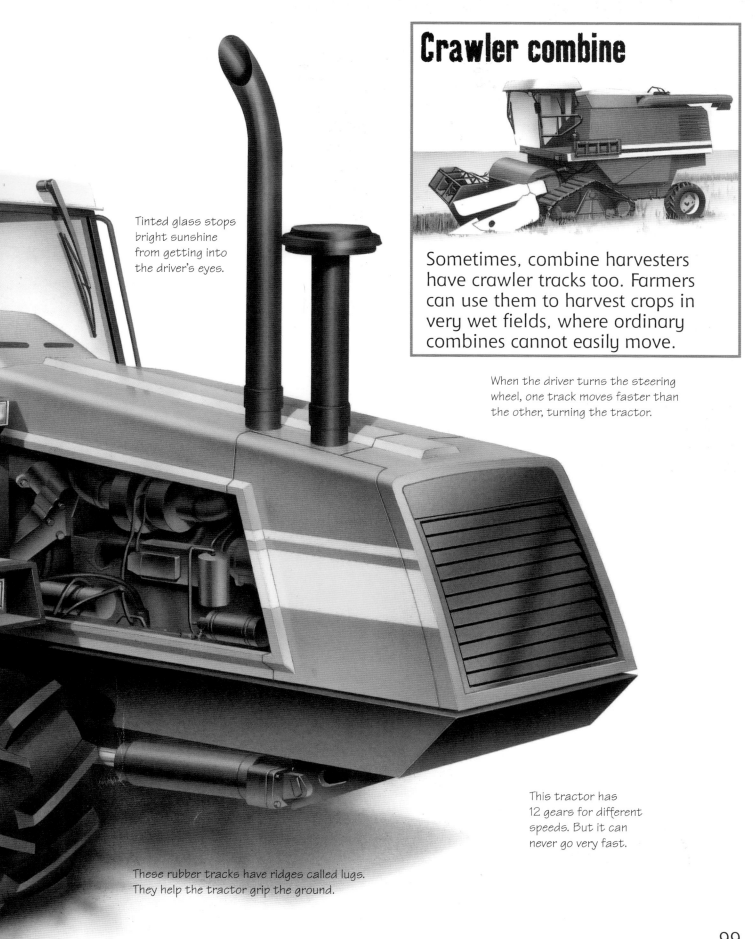

Tinted glass stops bright sunshine from getting into the driver's eyes.

Crawler combine

Sometimes, combine harvesters have crawler tracks too. Farmers can use them to harvest crops in very wet fields, where ordinary combines cannot easily move.

When the driver turns the steering wheel, one track moves faster than the other, turning the tractor.

This tractor has 12 gears for different speeds. But it can never go very fast.

These rubber tracks have ridges called lugs. They help the tractor grip the ground.

 # Special tractors

Farmers need different tractors for different jobs.

Three-wheeler

This tractor has three huge wheels. They hold so much air that the tractor doesn't squash the soil.

Its job is to spread fertilizer over big fields just before seeds are planted in them.

This tractor's cab is much higher above the ground than on ordinary tractors.

This light flashes when the tractor is moving on roads.

This trailer is full of fertilizer.

These giant wheels spread the tractor's weight over the field.

The engine is under the cab, not in front of it. This means that all three wheels help spread out its weight.

Mini-tractor

People use mini-tractors like this to mow the grass on golf courses, lawns and in parks. Sometimes they're called riding lawn mowers.

Narrow tractor

Narrow tractors like this can work between rows of grapevines or fruit trees, without damaging them.

This type of tractor is about half as wide as an ordinary tractor.

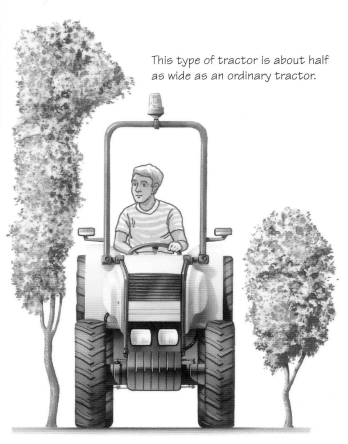

These wheels are more than twice as wide as ordinary tractor wheels.

ATV

Some farmers ride around their fields on bikes called ATVs, or All-Terrain Vehicles. They can go over any sort of ground.

Tractors old and new

Farming has changed a lot in the last 100 years. Tractors and other farming machines make the farmer's job much easier than it used to be.

Here you can see some of the earliest tractors, as well as other farm machines that are used today.

Early tractor

This tractor was built in Canada almost 100 years ago. At that time, more and more farmers were starting to use machines to do their farm-work.

This tractor used a fuel called kerosene.

These wheels are made of solid metal. They have ridges cut into them to help them to grip.

This type of tractor used petrol in its engine.

The Bull

This three-wheeled tractor was built in 1914. It was popular because it was tough and cheap to run.

Rubber wheels grip the ground better than metal.

Lighter tractor

By the 1930s, many tractors looked like this. They had rubber wheels rather than metal ones, making the tractor lighter and easier to drive.

Systems tractor

This machine works on many farms in Europe today. It is called a systems tractor.

Tools are fixed to the front, middle and back, so it can do three jobs at once.

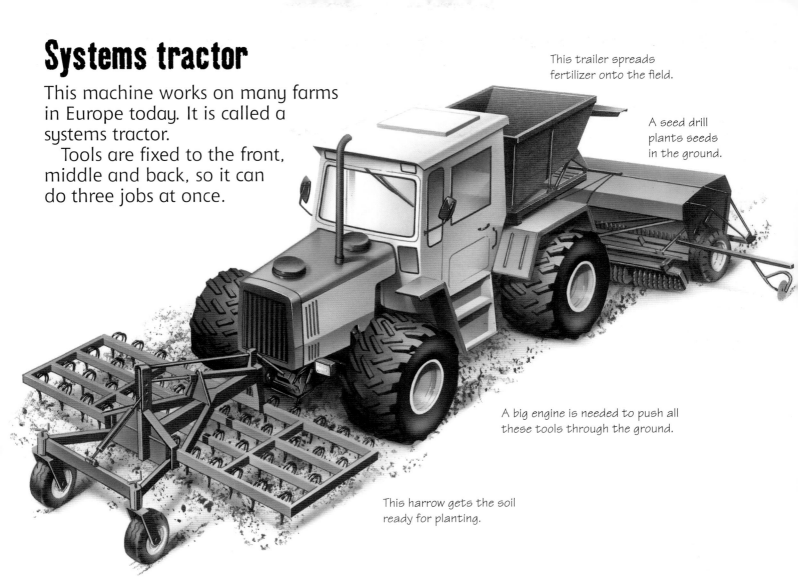

This trailer spreads fertilizer onto the field.

A seed drill plants seeds in the ground.

A big engine is needed to push all these tools through the ground.

This harrow gets the soil ready for planting.

Gantry

This wide machine farms big fields, as it can make fewer trips up and down. This stops it from squashing the soil.

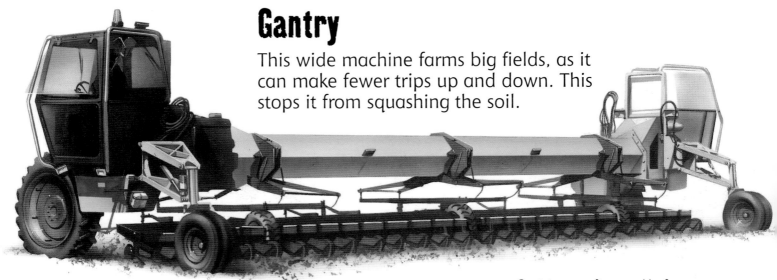

The driver has a clear view of the field and the gantry from the cab.

Some gantries are as long as six men lying down head to toe.

Gantries are often used by farmers who grow flowers. This sort of farming is called horticulture.

TRUCKS

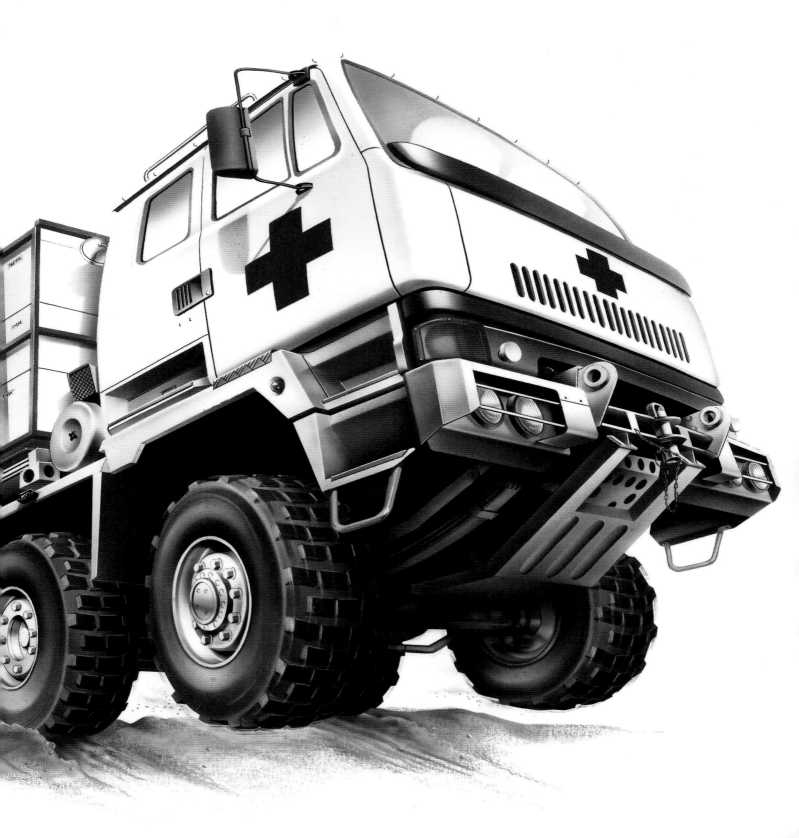

 # Trucks

Trucks are used for moving all sorts of things from one place to another. They often carry very heavy loads, so they need to have powerful engines and strong bodies.

Cab where the driver sits

The driver looks in the wing mirrors to see the road behind him.

The cab has a strong metal frame to protect the driver if there is an accident.

The front has been cut away so you can see the engine inside.

The headlights have their own wipers to keep them clean.

The wheels are big and wide to help carry the weight.

The body of the truck is where the load is put.

Different bodies

This truck's body is like a big box. It has extra space above the cab.

This truck's flat body is called a flatbed. The load goes on top.

The main frame of the truck is called the chassis. It is made of strong steel.

This truck has low sides that fold down to make unloading easier.

Engine check

Cab   Engine

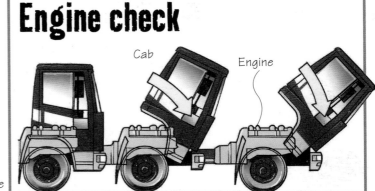

Double wheels at the back give extra support.

When the engine needs to be checked, the cab can be tilted forward. This makes the engine easy to reach.

Artics and rigid trucks

There are two main types of truck: articulated trucks, also called artics, and rigid trucks. Artics have two separate parts, which can be joined together and taken apart again. Rigid trucks are all in one piece.

Artic

The two parts of the artic are linked together. The cab at the front turns first when it goes around corners.

The part behind is called the semi-trailer. It can stand by itself when these metal legs are put down.

The semi-trailer locks onto a big metal plate here.

The front part of the artic is called the tractor unit.

Swapping semi-trailers

Tractor unit drives away.

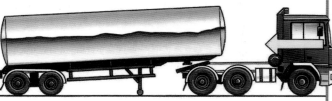

Tractor unit backs up to the new semi-trailer.

When the artic arrives at its destination, its two parts are disconnected. The semi-trailer is left behind to be unloaded.

A new semi-trailer is put on and the artic is ready to go. The driver can make lots more deliveries this way.

Curtainsider

A curtainsider is a rigid truck with sides that pull back like curtains.

A shaped panel at the front helps the truck push through the air when it is going fast.

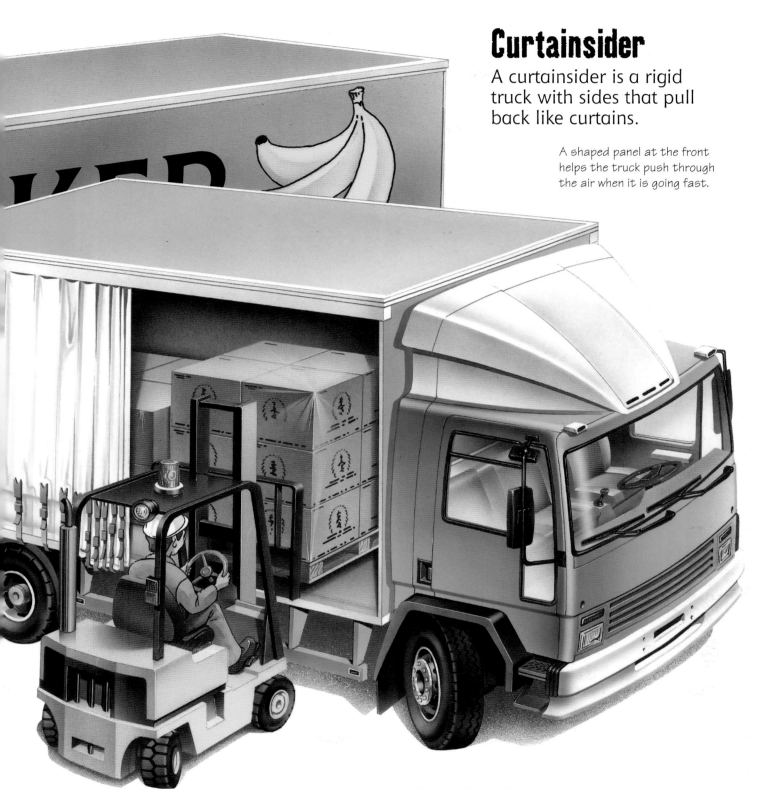

The curtains can be drawn back all the way along the sides.

Curtainsiders are easier to load because they open at the side. Most other trucks only open at the back.

Tankers can carry liquids, powders or gases. Many, like this tanker, are designed for carrying fuels.

The side of this tanker has been cut away so you can see inside.

There are separate compartments inside the tanker, so it can carry different loads at the same time. The compartments stop the liquid from sloshing around too much.

These curved sides are stronger than the flat sides on normal trucks.

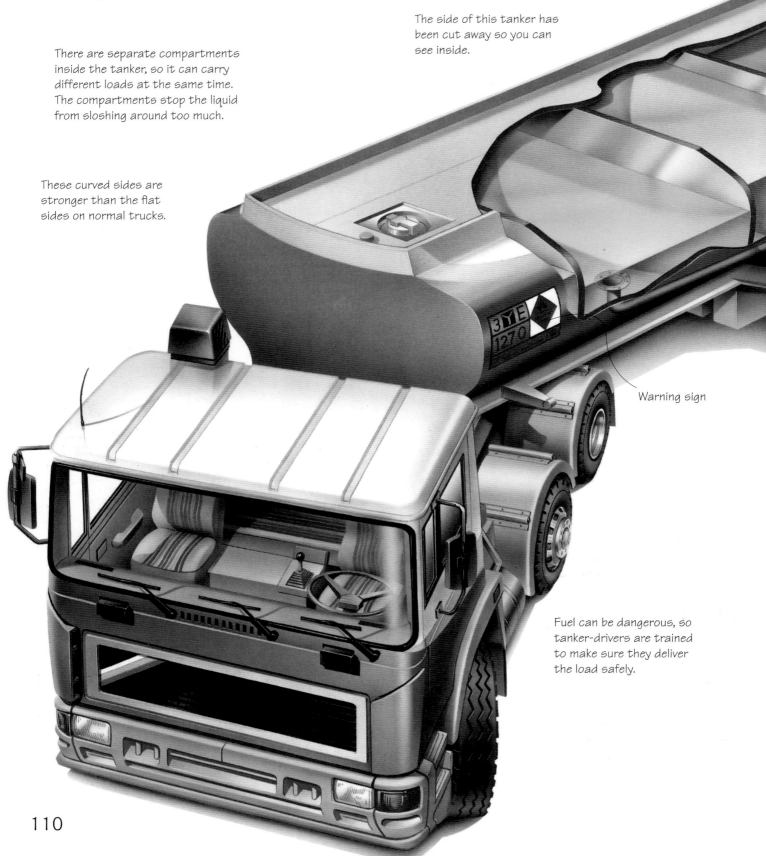

Warning sign

Fuel can be dangerous, so tanker-drivers are trained to make sure they deliver the load safely.

110

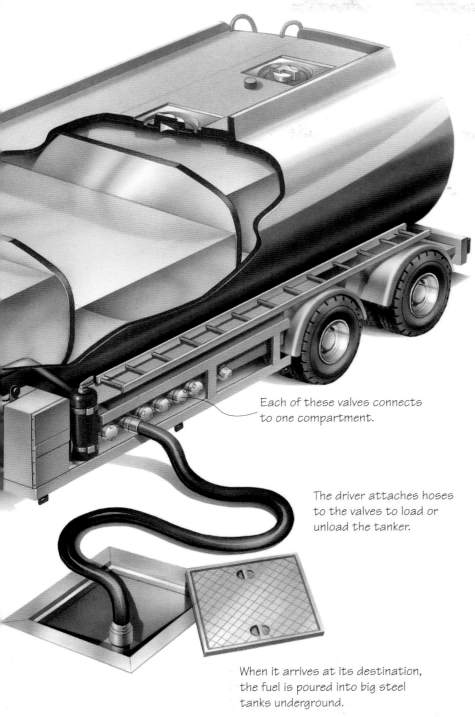

Each of these valves connects to one compartment.

The driver attaches hoses to the valves to load or unload the tanker.

When it arrives at its destination, the fuel is poured into big steel tanks underground.

Delivery

Hose

Storage tank

A hose from the tanker is put down into the storage tank. The fuel pours in.

Fuel pump

Fuel goes this way.

When someone uses the fuel pump, the fuel goes along a pipe and into the car's fuel tank.

Warning signs

Tankers have signs on them to show what's inside. Then, if the tanker catches fire, the firefighters will know how to deal with it.

FLAMMABLE LIQUID

FLAMMABLE SOLID

TOXIC GAS

A flammable liquid is one that can catch fire. This sign is used on fuel tankers.

This sign shows that the load is something solid that can catch fire.

This sign shows that the tanker is carrying a toxic, or poisonous, gas.

Dump truck

Dump trucks have bodies that tilt so that the load slides out. This giant dump truck is working at a quarry.

Dumping

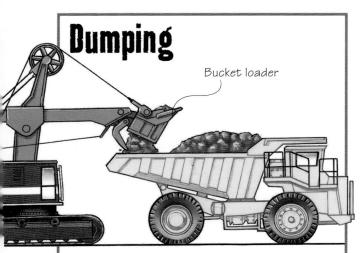

Bucket loader

The dump truck is filled with rocks by a big bucket loader.

Ram

To empty the dump truck, an arm called a ram lifts up the body. The load slides out.

Other dump trucks

Dump trucks of different sizes are used for carrying different loads. Sometimes smaller dump trucks are called tipper trucks. You can see three of them here.

This board protects the cab from falling rocks.

Exhaust pipes

The driver climbs this ladder to reach the cab.

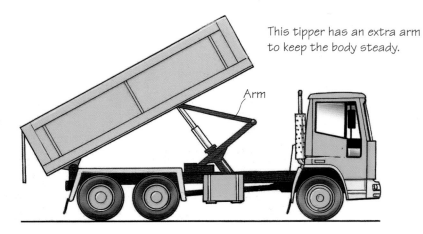

This tipper has an extra arm to keep the body steady.

Arm

Cab

This dump truck is too big to travel on normal roads. Its huge front wheels are as tall as an adult elephant.

The body of the dump truck is sloped at the bottom to stop the load from falling out when the truck is not dumping.

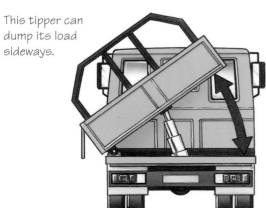

This tipper can dump its load sideways.

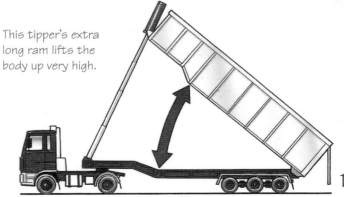

This tipper's extra long ram lifts the body up very high.

Tow truck

A tow truck is used when a car breaks down or has an accident.

The truck can lift the car back onto the road and then tow it away.

This arm is called a boom.

The driver works the winch with a control pad.

This cable is made of metal wire. It's very strong.

Metal rods called lifting rams hold the boom up.

Lights for working at night

These metal legs dig into the ground to help keep the truck still.

Muscle power

The first tow trucks carried only equipment. The crew did the lifting, with ropes, chains and a metal tripod.

Tripod

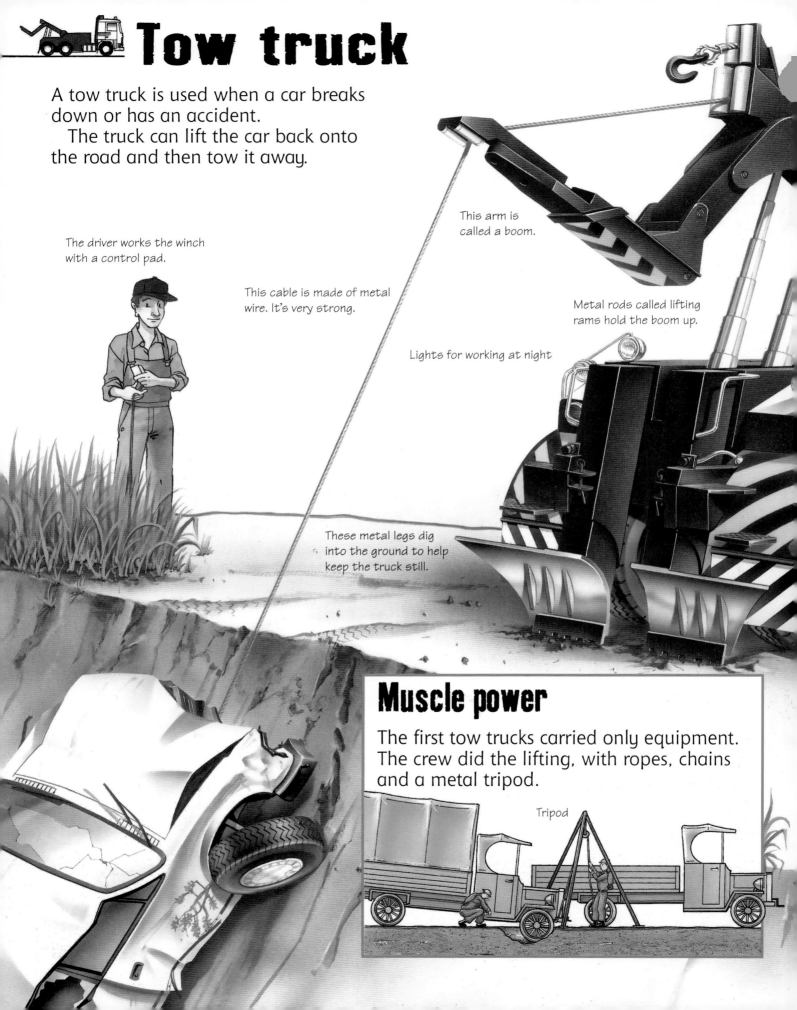

This drum is called a winch. It winds in the cable, pulling the car up.

Tools are kept in compartments at the side.

This truck can lift loads as heavy as 14 hippos.

Towing

A tow truck can tow things as big as itself, such as this bus.

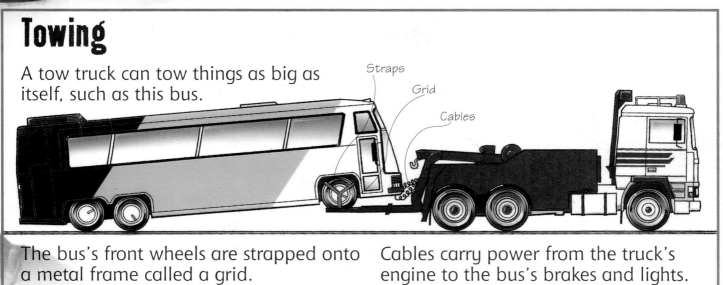

Straps

Grid

Cables

The bus's front wheels are strapped onto a metal frame called a grid.

Cables carry power from the truck's engine to the bus's brakes and lights.

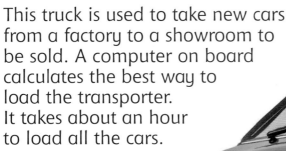 # Car transporter

This truck is used to take new cars from a factory to a showroom to be sold. A computer on board calculates the best way to load the transporter. It takes about an hour to load all the cars.

The driver has to be careful not to bash this car when turning corners.

Each car sits on a platform called a deck.

The cars are tied tightly to the decks with straps like seat belts.

The driver uses a ladder to reach up to the car above the cab.

116

Early transporter

This transporter was built in 1948. It could only carry four cars at a time.

The decks are tilted to fit the maximum number of cars onto the transporter. They are driven onto the transporter from the back.

The semi-trailer is very low to the ground so that more layers of cars can fit on.

Pro-jet truck

This racing truck is called a Pro-jet truck because it has a jet engine taken from a fighter plane. It is built for speed alone, so it isn't used for carrying loads like normal trucks.

The body of the truck carries the jet engine.

These tubes have parachutes inside. They open out to help the truck slow down.

The Pro-jet races on its own to see if it can beat speed records. It doesn't race with other trucks – it's about 100 times more powerful than a normal truck.

Truck racing

Sometimes the tractor units of normal trucks race against each other.

The drivers have to be very skilled to control the trucks when they are going fast.

The truck's top speed is about 240km/h (150mph). After going at top speed, it takes the truck about 500m (550yds) to be able to stop.

118

The driver wears a helmet and a special suit. They protect him if there is an accident.

This is an ordinary cab, but with extra panels attached. These help it push through the air at top speed.

119

Low-loader

A low-loader has a trailer that is low on the ground, making it easier to get the load on and off. That means it can carry very heavy things, like this excavator.

Bright stripes warn traffic that the truck is very long and wide.

Climbing on

Ramp

Chains

The excavator climbs up a ramp onto the trailer.

Then it turns on the spot to face the other way.

It is tied to the trailer with chains.

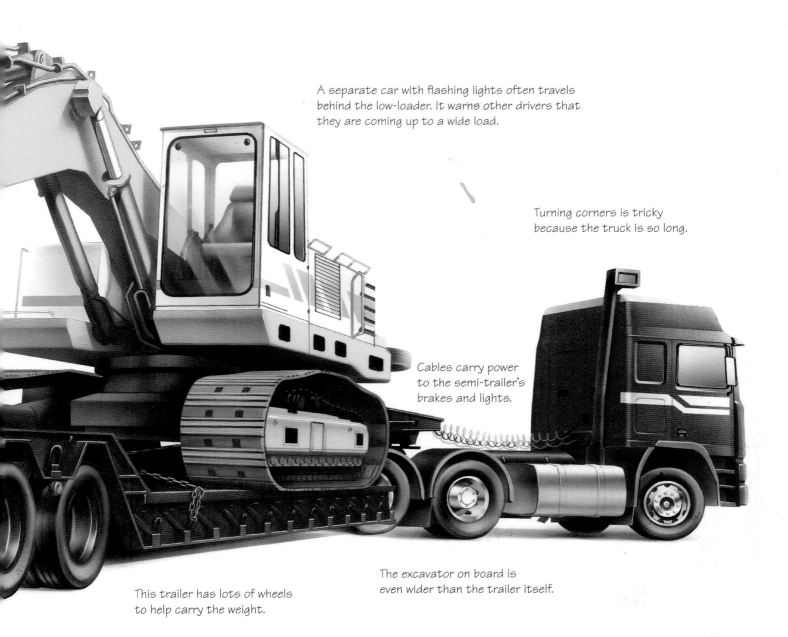

A separate car with flashing lights often travels behind the low-loader. It warns other drivers that they are coming up to a wide load.

Turning corners is tricky because the truck is so long.

Cables carry power to the semi-trailer's brakes and lights.

This trailer has lots of wheels to help carry the weight.

The excavator on board is even wider than the trailer itself.

Space Shuttle truck

One of the largest loads carried by a truck is this Space Shuttle orbiter. The truck drives it to the launching pad.

The truck is specially designed to take the orbiter. It's only used for this job.

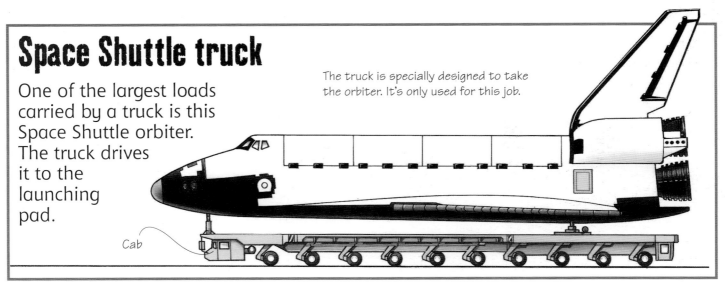

Cab

All-terrain truck

All-terrain trucks can drive over all sorts of ground without getting stuck. They have powerful engines and thick wheels. Their bodies are extra strong to stop them from getting damaged by rocky ground. This truck can load and unload itself, too.

An all-terrain truck can go up steep slopes, even with a heavy load.

The load sits on a frame called a rack.

Unloading

Arm

Rack

A metal arm lifts the rack and pushes it back until it touches the ground.

Arm

The truck drives out from underneath it.

Loading

To load again, the arm lifts up the rack and the truck drives back under it.

Then the arm pulls the rack up onto the truck's body and it is ready to drive away.

This truck is used to take medical supplies across a desert. For most of the way there are no paved roads.

This big cab has enough room for five people.

Bars at the front stop the headlights from getting smashed by rocks or stones.

The chassis is high off the ground so that it doesn't hit any rocks.

The eight wheels are big and wide. Their deep grooves help them grip wet and muddy ground.

 # Fire truck

Trucks are very important in firefighting. They rush the firefighters to the fire and they have all the equipment they need on board.

Fire trucks have loud sirens, to warn traffic on the roads to let them pass.

Special jobs

This all-terrain fire truck is used where driving is difficult, such as in thick forests and deserts.

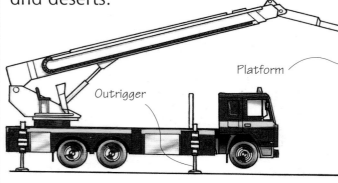

Platform

Outrigger

This fire truck raises and lowers a platform on its metal arm. It can reach up to the windows of tall buildings.

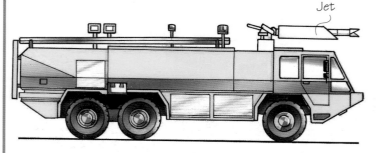

Jet

This fire truck stands by at the airport in case there is an accident. It has a strong water jet on the roof.

This arm can stretch up very high. Its bright lights help the firefighters if it is dark or smoky.

Hoses can be attached to each of the valves at the back.

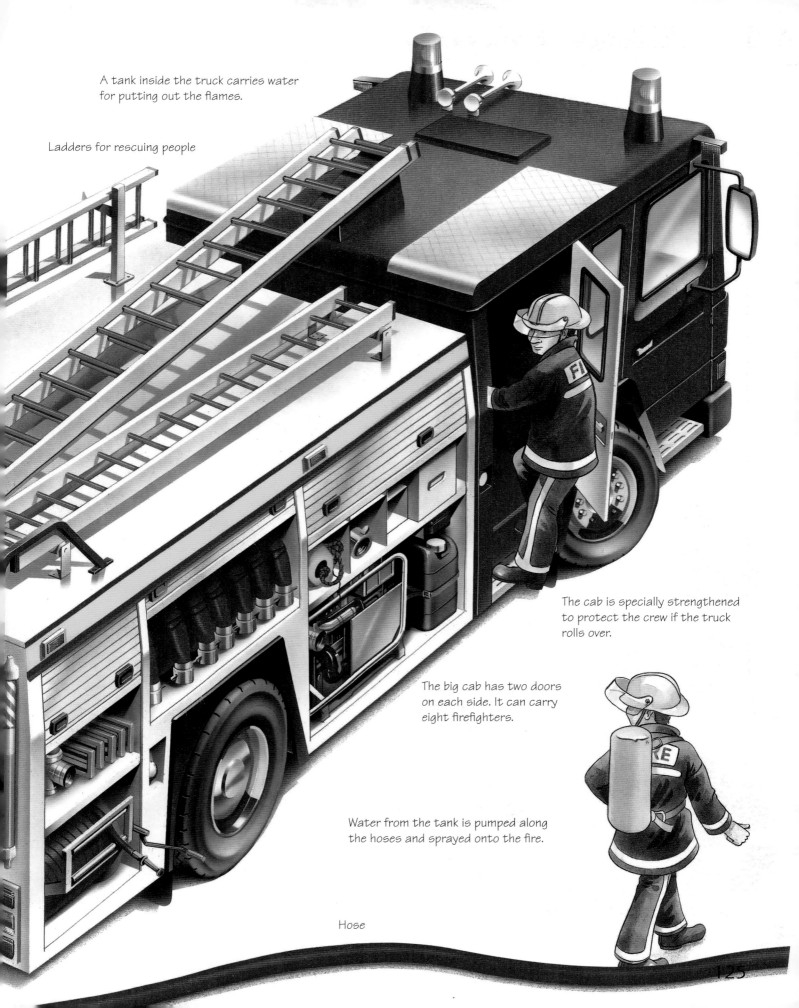

A tank inside the truck carries water for putting out the flames.

Ladders for rescuing people

The cab is specially strengthened to protect the crew if the truck rolls over.

The big cab has two doors on each side. It can carry eight firefighters.

Water from the tank is pumped along the hoses and sprayed onto the fire.

Hose

Snowblower

In winter, this truck helps clear the roads so that other traffic can get through. It churns up the snow and blows it onto the side of the road.

Powerful headlights help the driver see at all times.

The snow blows out of two chutes at the front.

A drum at the front turns around very fast. Its blades churn up the snow.

The snowblower has two engines. One drives the truck along and the other turns the drum.

As the truck moves along, it clears a path through the snow.

Chains stop the wheels from slipping on the snow.

Thick windows help block out noise from the engines and the blower.

How it works

Drum

The drum's blades cut into the snow. As they spin, they fling the snow up very hard.

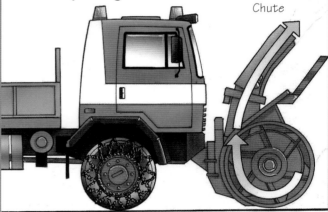

Chute

The snows flies out of the chutes. As the truck moves forward, it takes in more snow.

Snow breaker

A snow breaker clears snow by pushing it out of the way. It has a curved panel on the front called a face-plate.

Index